INSTITUTIONALIZATION OF THE ELDERLY IN CANADA

by

William F. Forbes and Jennifer A. Jackson

University of Waterloo

and

Arthur S. Kraus

Queen's University

Butterworths
Toronto and Vancouver

Institutionalization of the Elderly in Canada
© 1987 Butterworths, A division of Reed Inc.

Printed and bound in Canada

The Butterworth Group of Companies
Canada
Butterworths, Toronto and Vancouver
United Kingdom
Butterworth & Co. (Publishers) Ltd., London and Edinburgh
Australia
Butterworth Pty Ltd., Sydney, Melbourne, Brisbane, Adelaide and Perth
New Zealand
Butterworths (New Zealand) Ltd., Wellington and Auckland
Singapore
Butterworth & Co. (Asia) Pte. Ltd., Singapore
South Africa
Butterworth Publishers (SA) (Pty) Ltd., Durban and Pretoria
United States
Butterworth Legal Publishers, Boston, Seattle, Austin and St. Paul
D&S Publishers, Clearwater

Canadian Cataloguing in Publication Data
Forbes, William F. (William Frederick), 1924–
    Institutionalization of the elderly in Canada

(Perspectives on individual and population aging)
Bibliography: p.
Includes index.
ISBN 0-409-80522-X

1. Aged – Institutional care – Canada. 2. Long-
term care facilities – Canada. I. Jackson,
Jennifer A. II. Kraus, Arthur S. III. Title.
IV. Series.

HVI475.A2F67   1987   362.6'1'0971   C87-094530-0

Sponsoring Editor: Janet Turner
Executive Editor (P. & A.): Lebby Hines
Managing Editor: Linda Kee
Supervisory Editor: Marie Graham
Editor: Robert Goodfellow
Cover Design: Patrick Ng
Production: Jill Thomson

*To all those who work
with older adults to achieve
quality of life, and to our
families for their support and
encouragement, particularly to
our children for whom, when they
have become older adults,
this volume should be mainly of
historical interest because
of continued progress towards a
more rational approach.*

BUTTERWORTHS PERSPECTIVES ON INDIVIDUAL AND POPULATION AGING SERIES

The initiation of this Series represents an exciting and significant development for gerontology in Canada. Since the production of Canadian-based knowledge about individual and population aging is expanding rapidly, students, scholars and practitioners are seeking comprehensive yet succinct summaries of the literature on specific topics. Recognizing the common need of this diverse community of gerontologists, Janet Turner, Sponsoring Editor at Butterworths, conceived the idea of a series of specialized monographs that could be used in gerontology courses to complement existing texts and, at the same time, to serve as a valuable reference for those initiating research, developing policies, or providing services to elderly Canadians.

Each monograph includes a state-of-the-art review and analysis of the Canadian-based scientific and professional knowledge on the topic. Where appropriate for comparative purposes, information from other countries is introduced. In addition, some important policy and program implications of the current knowledge base are discussed, and unanswered policy and research questions are raised to stimulate further work in the area. The monographs have been written for a wide audience: undergraduate students in a variety of gerontology courses; graduate students and research personnel who need a summary and analysis of the Canadian literature prior to initiating research projects; practitioners who are involved in the daily planning and delivery of services to aging adults; and policy-makers who require current and reliable information in order to design, implement and evaluate policies and legislation for an aging population.

The decision to publish a monograph on a specific topic has been based in part on the relevance of the topic for the academic and professional community, as well as on the extent of information available at the time an author is signed to a contract. Thus, not all the conceivable topics are included in the early stages of the Series and some topics are published earlier rather than later. Because gerontology in Canada is attracting large numbers of highly qualified graduate students as well as increasingly active research personnel in academic, public and private settings, new areas of concentrated research will evolve. Hence, additional monographs that review and analyze work in these areas will be needed to reflect the evolution of knowledge on specialized topics pertaining to individual or population aging in Canada.

Before introducing the sixth monograph in the Series, I would like, on behalf of the Series' authors and the gerontology community, to acknowledge the following members of the Butterworths "team" and their respective staffs for their unique and sincere contribution to gerontology in Canada: Geoffrey Burn, President, for his continuing support of the project despite difficult times in the Canadian publishing industry; Janet Turner, Sponsoring Editor, for her vision, endurance and high academic standards; Linda Kee, Managing Editor, for her co-ordination of the production, especially her constant reminders to authors (and the Series Editor) that the hands of the clock continue to move in spite of our perceptions that manuscript deadlines were still months or years away; Jim Shepherd, Production Manager, for nimbly vaulting many a technical obstacle; and Gloria Vitale, Academic Sales Manager, for her support and promotion of the Series. For each of you, we hope the knowledge provided in this Series will have personal value — but not until well into the next century!

Barry D. McPherson
Series Editor

FOREWORD

In recent years it is unlikely that any other subject within gerontology has generated as much interest, and emotion, as matters pertaining to the institutionalization of elderly Canadians. To illustrate, four of the previous monographs in this Series have alluded, directly or indirectly, to demographic, cultural, ethnic, gender or drug concerns that relate to the institutionalized elderly. In general, the major topics of debate have included: the costs associated with institutionalizing the elderly compared with other alternatives; the emotional, decision-making process faced by the family as to whether, when and where an elderly relative should be institutionalized; the process and problems of adjusting to institutional living by elderly adults; the considerable variation in the quality of care provided in long-term care institutions; the inappropriate placement of elderly persons within institutionalized settings; and, most recently, the development and evaluation of facilities, programs and policies that can provide a continuum of care, ranging from community assistance for those who are capable of semi-independent living in their own home or apartment, to long-term institutional care for the frail elderly who have varying degrees of functional loss.

The trend toward caring for the elderly in long-term care institutions has been increasing in Canada in the past two decades — as of 1981, an estimated 209,000 Canadians aged sixty-five and over resided in long-term care institutions (see Table 2.5). Moreover, there are provincial variations in the rate of institutionalization (see Table 3.2), with Alberta having the highest rate (9.4%) and Newfoundland the lowest (5.6%).

Given this propensity to institutionalize elderly Canadians, this monograph provides a historical and contemporary review and critique of the existing research, policies, programs and practices related to the structure and operation of the long-term health-care system for elderly Canadians. The authors (a statistician, a physician now working in the field of education and an epidemiologist) have a long-standing and deep concern for the needs of elderly Canadians. This concern is illustrated by their review of the major issues faced, or not faced as yet, by the health-care system; by their critique of current scientific and policy knowledge; by their proposals for alternative models of assisting the frail elderly; and, by their attempts throughout the monograph to stimulate the reader to create, implement and evaluate alternative support services that will reverse and lower the trend toward unnecessary institutionalization. In short, the authors argue against the prevailing dichotomous model of social support and health care whereby most older individuals have only two choices — remain in one's home at increasing risk, or be relocated to a long-term care setting.

The monograph begins with a definition and description of the history of institutional care from early Christian and medieval times, to the earliest days of New France, to the 1980s in Canada. In Chapter 2, the reader is introduced to the organization and type of long-term care that is presently available in Canadian institutions for the elderly. Given the variation in jurisdictional responsibility across federal, provincial, regional and municipal boundaries, it is not surprising to learn that there is considerable variation across communities in the number of institutions available for the elderly, in the type and amount of community services provided to the elderly, and in the quality and cost of long-term institutional care. Chapter 3 presents a demographic profile of the institutionalized elderly in Canada, as well as comparisons with other countries. This chapter also identifies the sociodemographic and health factors that correlate with admission to an institutional facility.

In Chapter 4, the authors introduce a number of problematic issues that students, policy-makers, health professionals and practitioners need to understand and debate. A basic premise underlying the proposed solutions for these problems is that there should be an increase in the co-ordination of services between community and institutional agencies if the quality of care for elderly Canadians is to be enhanced. To illustrate, a number of outreach programs are described and their probable effectiveness for lowering admission rates and for enhancing the quality of care are discussed. There is also a need for new policies and practices within institutional settings. Thus, Chapter 5 stresses the importance of providing psychosocial care as well as medical and nursing care for such concerns as incontinence, falls and psychogeriatric problems. The authors also emphasize the need for a positive and flexible approach to institutional care that will enhance the independence of residents within the limits of their disabilities. They also note that, although many institutions are unable or unwilling to provide psychogeriatric, recreational or rehabilitation programs, some are initiating innovative programs and services that merit duplication and implementation elsewhere.

The final two chapters focus on neglected research and policy issues that should be addressed — the attitudes toward institutionalization held by the elderly, by staff and by policy-makers; the excessive medication of residents; the inappropriate placement of elderly persons; the need for staff development programs within long-term care institutions; the funding of services; the confusion and gaps created because of the multi-jurisdictional responsibility for care of the elderly; the variation in the quality of care; and, the development and implementation of community-based preventive measures to lower the onset and rate of institutionalization. Some of these issues, and their proposed solutions, are controversial and the authors are to be commended for addressing and proposing radical and innovative solutions to complex problems. However, even if viable alternatives are available for experimentation and evaluation, existing policies will continue to serve as guidelines unless practitioners and innovative policy-makers express a willingness to consider and try more cost-effective and humane policies and practices. These new initiatives are especially important for the frail elderly who need to live in some type of communal residential setting. Therefore, the authors and I urge the concerned reader to seriously consider and debate the problems and proposed solutions presented in this monograph; to question the status quo with respect to institutionalization policies and practices within your community and province; and, to develop, experiment with, and evaluate alternative policies and procedures for providing social support and health-care assistance to older Canadians.

Barry D. McPherson, Ph.D.
Series Editor
Waterloo, Ontario, Canada
July 1987

PREFACE

The object of this monograph is to provide information regarding the care of elderly people in long-term care institutions in Canada. In keeping with the general direction of the Series, it will aim to provide an up-to-date view of the topic, of use to students, teachers, policymakers, professionals and laypeople when working with and for aging adults.

The range of institutional care available in Canada and in other countries results in difficulties when classifying types of institutions, which may overlap in their functions and services. Problems also arise in establishing accurate, comparative statistics of the number and proportion of elderly people who are institutionalized. These numbers, as well as the future demographic trends, have been of concern to many in recent years, both for humanitarian and for financial reasons. Opinions have been expressed that institutional care is frequently an inappropriate and costly way to provide needed support. Although innovative, responsive centres exist in many countries, including Canada, a negative connotation is often associated with institutions caring for the elderly. Inappropriate placement of the individual in long-term care and the popular attitude that institutional placement is the end of the road, with a loss of personal freedom and identity for the resident, have combined to encourage these negative perceptions. Admission to institutional care, at one level or another, has been a solution too easily accepted when an elderly person can no longer manage independently in his or her home.

It is recognized now that institutional care is not the only option for the frail elderly, many of whom can be supported in their own home or while living with relatives. On the other hand, institutional care for some individuals may be the most appropriate and cost-effective option, which provides a happy and fulfilling, yet supportive environment. Moreover, the availability of institutional care is an important factor in the provision of community care. It is a part of, but not necessarily the final stage in, the continuum of care. Professional workers, families and the elderly themselves, need the assurance that institutional care will be available if family and community service support are no longer adequate to meet the individual's needs, whether on a temporary or permanent basis.

Determining the nature and role of institutional care must incorporate the view of the elderly, their families, professional workers of various disciplines and society in general. The elderly are not a homogeneous group, and their needs differ. What is suitable for one area and group of individuals may not be appropriate elsewhere. Further, an elderly person's needs change, often rapidly, and various levels of care, in institutions as well as in the community, may be needed at different times. The change may not necessarily involve increasing degrees of assistance. Indeed, the need for extra help may result from a change in the situation of caregivers, such as the family. Accurate and repeated assessment of the level of function and matching this with the appropriate level of care, are important for the best use of services and for the provision of optimal assistance to the elderly.

Institutions in some form are here to stay — communal, supportive, caregiving environments are needed for some elderly individuals. The challenge is to develop establishments which can provide in a communal setting the appropriate range of social, psychological and medical care to those who need such help, while maintaining personal choice, freedom, dignity and integrity to the greatest extent possible. At the same time, institutions and those who live and work there, should be part of the community as a whole, just as they are part of the continuum of care, and should not be isolated as the final phase of care.

The general perspective of the monograph is to present the basic information and informed opinion which is needed to understand the nature and operation of the system for long-term institutional care of the elderly in Canada, the relationship between that system and other sources of care for the elderly, the issues and problems confronting the system, and the forces and directions of change in that system now and in the foreseeable future. Chapter 1 provides a definition of institutional care and outlines the history of such care. Chapter 2 addresses the present organization of institutional long-term care in Canada and discusses the various types of available facilities, and the populations for which these institutions are designed. Following this, Chapter 3 discusses the demographics of the institutionalized elderly, how the prevalence of institutionalization among the elderly in Canada compares with the prevalence in other jurisdictions, and aims to identify some of the factors associated with admission to long-term care institutions. For brevity, both Chapters 2 and 3 emphasize the situation in Ontario, although reference is also made to the provision of institutional long-term care in other provinces. Having thus summarized the present situation of institutional care in Canada, Chapter 4 outlines some issues concerning the interface between community-oriented services and institutions and specifically discusses community-based programs which may prevent, or at least delay, institutionalization. Chapter 5 deals with the health and functional abilities of the elderly and with programs which may be needed for the care of the long-stay elderly resident. Chapter 6 addresses sources of concern, that is, issues for which there seems to be scope for substantial improvement, such as attitudes towards institutionalization, excessive medication, inappropriate placement and divided jurisdictional responsibility. Unfortunately, there are probably no simple solutions. This chapter also includes a discussion of some methodological considerations, emphasizing that much of the information which one would like to have is not available. It also stresses that evaluations of what is available should be regarded as a priority. Finally, in Chapter 7, some problem areas are outlined which could benefit from appropriate research; these are the quality and outcomes of care and the implications of government policy and programs. Also, attempts are made to identify aspects which are likely to alter in the future, such as the incidence of diseases affecting the elderly. It is stressed that little is known about what is likely to happen to the average life span and to health in later years, although such changes may have a major effect on the institutionalization of the elderly.

In a monograph of this type, it is not possible to cover all aspects of the subject and it was not the intention to do so. The topics which have been selected are the ones which may be of particular interest to individuals who are working with the elderly, or areas in which major changes are likely to occur in the near future.

The authors would like to acknowledge the assistance of many colleagues who provided valuable comments; Drs. Lynn Beattie, Neena Chappell, Barry McPherson, Cope Schwenger, Mrs. Lauranna M. Jones and Mr. John Hirdes were particularly helpful in this regard. In addition, the comments from staff at Butterworths, particularly those of Mr. Robert Goodfellow and Ms. Janet Turner are appreciated. The excellent technical assistance provided by Mrs. Jacqueline Macpherson and Mrs. Helen Warren is gratefully acknowledged; without their competent and dedicated efforts, this monograph would not have been completed in time.

CONTENTS

TABLES

CHAPTER 1

INTRODUCTION

1.1 THE DEFINITION OF INSTITUTIONAL CARE

This monograph discusses the provision of care in residential settings for the elderly. Such facilities are generally intended to provide twenty-four-hour accommodation, food services, and various degrees of care and treatment. These institutions could include acute and psychiatric hospitals, but the term institutionalization, or institutional care, as it pertains to the elderly, is usually reserved for long-term care. This has been defined (Ontario Hospital Association 1980) as care

> ... provided on a sustained and prolonged basis to meet the physical, social and personal needs of individuals whose functional capacities are chronically impaired or at risk of impairment. It implies a team approach which utilizes the skills of physcians, nurses, social workers, behavioural scientists, physical therapists, nutritionists and others in an effort to treat social-psychological as well as physical disabilities.

Care of the elderly in acute or psychiatric hospitals, although it may involve problems special to old age, is not discussed here in any detail. On the other hand, the definition of institution is not limited to facilities which might be viewed as "total institutions" (Goffman 1961), where the authority of the staff is paramount and the interests of the client (the patient) tend to be subservient to those of the organization.

A variety of names and definitions are applied to institutions providing long-term care for the elderly, but within Canada common terms are: chronic care hospital, nursing home, home for the aged, special care or personal care home and residential or rest home. Although institutions are often regarded as relatively large residential facilities with twenty-five or more beds, many may be smaller than this, particularly retirement homes providing low levels of care.

While the distinction between residing in the "community" and in an "institution" may be related to the difference between those who are healthy and those who are ill, or between those able to care for themselves and those "dependent" on the care of others, these groupings are not exclusive. In general the elderly residents of institutions have some degree of dependency and have one or more chronic illnesses or disabilities, but many are relatively independent. Conversely, many disabled and sick elderly individuals remain at home, since long-term care is not confined to institutions. The community provision of long-term care, however, is not discussed here, except where it overlaps with that provided within residential facilities (see Chapter 4). Nor are community settings such as congregate or sheltered housing for the elderly discussed, as they are not usually regarded as providing the degree of organized care associated with an "institution."

1.2 THE HISTORY OF INSTITUTIONAL CARE

Relatively little has been written about the history of institutional care of the elderly in Canada. Indeed, for many centuries there was virtually no care specifically for aged members of the population in this or in other countries, such as France, England and the United States. The poor and sick elderly were not seen as a distinct group, but as part of other disadvantaged groups. In order to understand the development of, and attitudes towards institutional care in Canada, it is worth tracing the history of society's efforts to care for the sick, the poor, the elderly and other destitute individuals.

1.2.1 Early Christian and Medieval Periods

Throughout history the first recourse for those in need has been the family. Whether sick, disabled, poor, mentally ill or in any other way incapacitated, an individual would turn first to his or her family, and it was considered the family's duty to provide whatever help could be managed. Yet there were always those who did not have this help available. In these cases, the local community or a charitable-minded individual might take on the responsibility of providing the necessities of life. The Christian Church in what is now the Middle East set up institutions during the third and fourth centuries to care for those in need. According to E. D. Churchill (quoted in Townsend 1962, 17), these institutions were differentiated in their functions; *Gerontochia* existed for the elderly, *Nosochomia* for the sick, *Ptochia* for the poor. Gradually, similar places were established by monastic groups in Western Europe. By medieval times, however, the roles of these different institutions had become blurred and, in the infirmary almshouses and Houses of Pity which existed at that time, various needs were met, regardless of age or physical condition.

1.2.2 England and Wales

With the dissolution of the monasteries in the sixteenth century, such sources of help disappeared in England and Wales, though this pattern of care continued elsewhere in Europe. Responsibility for the poor was taken on by the parishes and, under the Poor Relief Act of 1601, "Poor Houses" were established to house the blind, sick, disabled, mentally ill and destitute, both young and old. Mixed custodial institutions were the accepted way to look after those who were unable, for some reason, to care for themselves, and parish poorhouses existed in various sizes across England and Wales. Also known as workhouses, they were used to obtain labour from the unemployed, but a report in the 1830s estimated that a third to a half of the sixty to eighty occupants of a typical parish workhouse were "aged and impotent persons" (Townsend 1962, 18).

The Poor Law Amendment Act of 1834 grouped parishes into Unions under the supervision of elected Boards of Guardians, who reported to a Central Board of Poor Law Commissioners. The work of the Commissioners were directed primarily towards the able-bodied poor, and was guided by the principle that the conditions of life provided by public relief should be less pleasant than those experienced by workers of the lowest class in the community. This attitude arose both from a wish to dissuade individuals from turning to public relief and from the belief that those in need were largely to blame for their situation (Townsend 1962, 20–22). Indeed, it has been said that a major reason for the establishment of poorhouses, or Houses of Industry, with their deliberately undesirable conditions and strict discipline, was to induce an unwilling population to enter the growing industrial labour force on any terms (Myles 1980, 263–64).

Although classification of the institutions had been recommended, in practice the system of housing all the destitutes of society in one institution, continued. Indeed, ease of administration and economy led to the construction of relatively large institutions serving a wider geographical area than previously, with the result that, by 1839, the average workhouse contained two hundred paupers – old and young, sick and able-bodied. However, Thomson (1983, 46) has shown that in the middle decades of the nineteenth century, the aged formed a minority of most workhouse populations, and not until the last years of that century did official documents make anything but passing reference to the elderly occupants of the workhouse and their special needs. Although it was accepted that some of these old people were "deserving" and "of blameless character," the attitude remained that many elderly, like the able poor, were in the workhouse because they had led dissolute or improvident lives (Townsend 1962, 20–23).

1.2.3 Care of the Sick Poor

For the sick, including the frail elderly, there was little choice in the early nineteenth century but the poorhouse if they did not have the family to provide care, or the money to employ someone. The founding of voluntary hospitals in the eighteenth and nineteenth centuries provided relatively few beds. Furthermore, as medical knowledge and the number of hospitals expanded in the nineteenth century, emphasis was placed on the treatment of the acutely sick, rather than on those who were chronically ill (Abel-Smith 1960, 2–3). As in more recent decades, care of the chronic sick held little attraction for the medical profession. Only a few of the sick elderly were admitted to the new hospitals because their cases were of interest to those involved in teaching or research, or because they were fortunate enough to receive the support and recommendation of one of the hospitals' subscribers.

In general, any care provided in the workhouse for the sick and frail was by "pauper nurses," that is, able-bodied inmates who were required to provide assistance to the infirm, often without pay, although extra rations or spirits might be provided. This situation was not unusual since, until the 1830s, all nurses were untrained and often illiterate. The antecedents of the nursing profession were domestic servants, and in the first half of the nineteenth century nurses were assigned few of the tasks later regarded as nursing duties. Experience gained as a domestic servant, or in looking after her own family, was considered to be adequate for the nurse, although some acquired practical knowledge and skills from the doctor with whom they worked. In the workhouses many of the pauper nurses would themselves be elderly. Of eighteen pauper nurses at the Strand Workhouse in the 1860s, fourteen were over sixty, and four were over seventy (Abel-Smith 1960, 9, 11). Where non-pauper nurses were employed in the workhouse, they tended to be the least experienced and least desirable individuals.

1.2.4 Canada – New France

Canada's institutions and policies for the relief of its poor and sick were influenced by the background of the country's earliest European settlers. The emphasis in the early history of public welfare in Canada was on the relief of poverty and aid for the sick, with little distinction by age. In the seventeenth century, individuals continued with their occupation throughout life, even into old age. For the elderly who were unable to continue working, it was expected that they had set aside adequate resources or that relatives would provide support. In New France the pattern of aid for those in need during the seventeenth century followed that of France, where the Church continued to be primarily responsible. One hospital was established in Quebec in 1639 and another in Montreal in 1644 (Strong 1930, 13). Support from France, however, seems to have been temporary or very limited for, in 1687, a plea was sent from the colonies on behalf of the hospitals (Clark 1942, 49).

Poverty appears to have been a persistent problem. Bureaux des Pauvres were opened in 1688 at Quebec, Three Rivers and Montreal to identify and assist "the unfortunate poor, aged and truly destitute invalids" (Clark 1942,

48). However, eventually the authorities, with the agreement of the King, resorted to an institutional solution to the problem of preventing "the idleness of poor beggars." With the object of "relieving the destitute sick and invalids and those people not able to subsist by their own labour" (Clark 1942, 50), religious communities established "general hospitals" at Quebec in 1692, Ville-Marie on the island of Montreal in 1694 and Three Rivers in 1702 (Strong 1930, 14). These institutions resembled the English workhouse in that those able to do so were expected to work, but they also followed the pattern established earlier by religious communities in Europe by providing care for the sick and disabled.

1.2.5 Lower Canada

During the early years of British rule in Canada, attention was directed mainly towards keeping order, and there is no reference in offical reports of relief for the poor and sick other than "the loan of seeds for corn and other necessaries" (Strong 1930, 16). The care of the indigent sick, the insane and foundlings in Lower Canada continued to be undertaken by private philanthropy and by the Roman Catholic Church.

To extend this work and to support the hospitals already established, it became necessary to provide additional public support, and in 1801 the provincial legislature appropriated one thousand pounds per annum for three years to help religious foundations caring for foundlings, the sick and the infirm. In 1804 this grant was renewed, and continued thereafter with periodic increases in the amount. A house of industry, established in Montreal through a bequest, was incorporated in 1818 by the legislature of Lower Canada. However, although the charities receiving subsidies had to account for the way the money was used, there was no attempt at government control through regulations or standards. Only in 1823 was there reference to the appointment of commissioners who were responsible for reporting the expenditure of grant money (Strong 1930, 20, 36). Appointment of these commissioners, although with limited powers, gave some recognition to the concept of the state's responsibility for the care of the insane and sick.

1.2.6 Upper Canada

In Upper Canada, it was not the Church but municipal councils which provided relief for the destitute. However, in this pioneer, rural society, those who had established themselves and their families successfully had little patience for those who had failed to do so and, in keeping with this, local officials emphasized self-reliance and foresight. Welfare, therefore, was not easy to obtain, and municipal councils required a careful scrutiny of an applicant's economic assets, earning possibilities and morals before providing assistance. One method of providing assistance was the practice of "auctioning off" the able-bodied poor who were without relatives in the area (Johnson 1973, 255). When such an individual applied for help, the Council would offer that person as a boarder for the lowest bid. Even an elderly person, if in good health, could be useful in a household with many young children. Although the treatment of these individuals was sometimes bad, the practice was accepted in the community, and any objection by the person involved would have resulted in the withdrawal of all assistance.

If the situation of the able-bodied poor was often less than satisfactory, that of the bedridden, senile and mentally ill who had no relatives to care for them, was worse. With no formal provision for such people, they often became residents of the local jail (Johnson 1973, 258). This situation did cause concern among officials, but suggestions to build a poorhouse or House of Refuge were usually rejected as a needless expense. The attitude that destitution was the result of a wasted life seems to have been as strong in North America as in Victorian England. Fischer (1978, 60–61) has suggested that, although there was respect for age in early American society when it concerned powerful, prosperous men, to be old and poor was to be despised. Ships arriving at New England ports were searched for "old persons," as well as "maimed, lunatic ... or vagrant persons," who were then sent away to prevent an increase of pauperism in the colony. Similar concerns were expressed in Nova Scotia, and there is at least one record of twenty "mostly old" people being returned to the British Isles because the town was unable to maintain them (Clark 1942, 129). Even widows of the community, if they were old, poor or without supporting relatives, were sometimes driven away by their neighbours who feared an increase in the poor rates (Fischer 1978, 63). Such events may be extreme examples, but they illustrate the attitudes current in the eighteenth and early nineteenth centuries.

In time, however, growth in the urban areas of Upper Canada, a fluctuating economy and seasonal unemployment led to such suffering and destitution among the urban poor that, in 1830, provincial grants were made to the York Hospital and the Female Benevolent Society of Kingston for the care of the destitute sick. In 1837, the government of Upper Canada passed legislation which permitted the building and maintenance of a house of industry in the province at public expense, and Toronto was given a grant of two hundred and fifty pounds "for the relief of the poor and distressed" (Strong 1930, 25, 27–28). Five inspectors were appointed with power to inspect and govern the house and to appoint the necessary staff. There is no indication whether the staff were sufficient to provide adequate care for the sick and feeble or whether, as in the English workhouse, much of the care was provided by other inmates. Certainly the intent of the house of industry was to provide employment for the indigent and idle, and there was no distinction by age in the criteria for admission.

1.2.7 Developments During 1840–1900

During the mid-nineteenth century many charitable organizations were incorporated in the Province of Canada. Some dispensed "outdoor relief" in the form of food and clothing, but most established homes for orphans, destitute widows or the infirm and aged, often with the idea of combining relief with moral and religious instruction. Many of these institutions received grants but initially there was little or no provision for inspection (Strong 1930, 35, 46). While in England stricter administration of the Poor Law Acts was being introduced, in Canada the care of the sick and poor remained subject to local or private initiative. Although many of the associated attitudes and beliefs existed in Canada, the Poor Law itself was not instituted in Upper or Lower Canada, and legislation enabled rather than required the establishment of poorhouses. Both Nova Scotia and New Brunswick, however, instituted a Poor Law in the late eighteenth century which required municipalities to provide relief and support to all indigent residents (Morgan 1980, 87).

As in the workhouses of England, conditions in a house of industry did not encourage residents to stay, and admission was often considered a disgrace. Those sent there were expected to work and could be punished if they were idle or disorderly. The house of industry, therefore, became largely a refuge for the poor and infirm elderly of the district, or a shelter for the disabled or temporarily unemployed. Between 1867 and 1870, a severe depression caused widespread unemployment and poverty in the province of Ontario, and the government introduced legislation which would have required counties to build houses of refuge. Strong opposition from rural areas, however, led to the proposal for mandatory legislation being dropped (Johnson 1973, 261), and only permissive legislation was passed (Passmore 1967). Nevertheless, the county of Norfolk in Ontario established a house of industry which admitted its first inmate in October 1868, and the following year, a county poorhouse and farm was established by Waterloo. Other counties followed this example, with the financial burden being shared with the municipalities (Strong 1930, 121). However, by 1890 only seven more county houses had been opened. Provincial legislation, therefore, was passed in 1890 which provided grants to counties for the purchase of land and the construction of a house of refuge. This Act also provided for inspection of houses of refuge by the provincial Inspector of Prisons and Public Charities. Previously, county councils had been responsible for the inspection of municipal houses. Charitable institutions had been provincially inspected since 1868 (Passmore 1967).

Thus, society's response to the elderly's problems of poverty, feebleness and illness was the same as that for other age groups, and involved segregation in large comfortless institutions.[1] As in England, there was little or no systematic classification of those in need of care. Although during the nineteenth century foundlings and the insane were seen as distinct groups and separate institutions were established for them, the elderly continued to be crowded together with the poor sick, the disabled, widows, vagrants and drunkards, unless they were senile, in which case they were likely to be sent to the insane asylum.

1.2.8 The Period from 1900 to the 1940s

Up to 1900 the history of institutional long-term care in Canada is repre-sented by developments in Quebec, Ontario and two of the Atlantic Prov-inces, Nova Scotia and New Brunswick. In Quebec, private rather than public initiative remained almost universal, in spite of powers granted by the Municipal Code (1881) and the Cities and Towns Acts (1903) which per-mitted councils to establish houses of refuge, to support hospitals and other charitable institutions, and to support the old and infirm. The permissive legislation of Ontario regarding houses of refuge must be contrasted with the Poor Law enacted in Nova Scotia and New Brunswick, which required municipalities to provide relief for all indigent residents and established control over the poorhouses (Clark 1942, 134–35; Morgan 1980, 87). By 1926, twenty-four poorhouses existed in Nova Scotia, and a government inspector, who was a physician, had the power to make regulations regard-ing the diet, clothing and bedding of the patients, as well as their employ-ment, conduct and punishment (Strong 1930, 149–50).

In the western provinces the Poor Law was not enacted and assistance for the needy was organized locally through neighbourly action, with varying degrees of municipal responsibility (Morgan 1980, 87). Long-term care facilities for the elderly in the western provinces developed slowly after the turn of the century. In Saskatchewan, for example, the first long-term care facilities were built in the late 1920s. They were small, usually run by local church congregations, and emphasized independent living, although a few provided some nursing care. By the early 1940s there were only six homes for the aged, accommodating about three hundred and fifty people (Stolee et al. 1981, 6).

In Ontario there were seventy-six houses of refuge by the mid-1920s, forty-five being city institutions. These catered largely to the poor elderly. They received both municipal and provincial grants, and were government inspected, but were administered by private boards. Uniform standards among the institutions were not possible, although regulations had to be approved by the lieutenant-governor in council (Strong 1930, 116, 124–29). Efforts were being made to establish some exchange of information between institutions, for example through the Ontario Association of Managers of Homes for the Aged and Infirm, but a custodial attitude towards the residents remained and there was little or no attempt to assess their differing needs or to establish therapeutic programs. Similar conditions and attitudes remained until after the Second World War.

There is little published information about the inmates of houses of refuge, their length of stay or standards of care and treatment. The inspector of prisons and public charities in Ontario reported that 2,345 males and 3,420 females had been cared for in city houses of refuge during 1925, while the average daily population of county houses was 1,852 in 1926. The cost of maintaining an individual in these institutions varied. The inspector reported a range of twenty-four cents to $2.25 per day in 1925, with an average cost of eighty-eight cents in the city refuges. Provincial grants were made at the rate of ten cents for each day's maintenance of an indigent person (Strong 1930, 124, 128–30).

Statistics regarding the number of adults under care in charitable and benevolent institutions were first collected by the Dominion Bureau of Statistics in 1931. In June 1941 there were one hundred and sixty homes for adults across Canada and another ninety-eight which housed adults and children, the latter term including minors under twenty years of age. These institutions provided custodial care to dependent and handicapped people and, according to *The Canada Year Book 1943–44*, included "all homes for the care of the aged and indigent, refuges, asylums ..." (Canada, Dominion Bureau of Statistics 1944, 677). Of 16,523 adults under care, 68.7% were aged sixty years or older (see Table 1.1). Among all the institutionalized adults, 21% (3,474) were classed as "harmlessly insane, feeble-minded, or subnormal," and 11.2% (1,855) were blind, deaf and dumb, or crippled. Ten years later, in 1951, there were 18,597 adults under care in charitable, benevolent and welfare institutions (Canada, Dominion Bureau of Statistics 1954, 264).

In addition to the custodial houses of refuge and the acute care hospitals, a growing need for convalescent and chronic care beds had been noted by the end of the nineteenth century. Improvements in public health measures and advances in medical science resulted in a higher proportion of the population living to old age, often with concomitant disability or chronic illness. Unfortunately, lack of interest by the medical profession and the community led, for a long time, to insufficient beds, services and facilities specifically designed for such patients (Agnew 1974, 203–6). In some cases a convalescent or chronic care unit occupied one section of a general hospital, which facilitated the transfer of patients. Other convalescent and chronic care facilities were built as separate institutions, often away from the city centre and patterned after tuberculosis sanitoria. The earliest was built in Toronto in 1886, and by the 1920s there were more than fifty institutions across Canada, providing about 2,500 chronic care and convalescent beds. Although the statistics may be incomplete, there seem to have been about 31 voluntary and 136 private hospitals or nursing homes by 1942. Services and standards provided by these institutions varied. Some, in centres such as Montreal, Toronto and Winnipeg, were well equipped and provided good treatment and care but others, according to Agnew, did not deserve to be called hospitals. Many of the private facilities provided little more than

TABLE 1.1

ADULTS IN CARE, BY PROVINCES, 1941[1]

Item		P.E.I.	N.S.	N.B.	Que.	Ont.	Man.	Sask.	Alta.	B.C.	Total
Totals, Adults in Care all ages	M	98	826	155	2,718	2,982	158	154	123	340	7,554
	F	120	1,000	295	4,043	2,766	201	93	57	394	8,969
	T	218	1,826	450	6,761	5,748	359	247	180	734	16,523
Age Groups											
60–69 years	M	24	152	39	842	956	9	33	4	88	2,147
	F	12	157	49	758	550	8	10	16	31	1,591
	T	36	309	88	1,600	1,506	17	43	20	119	3,738
70 years or over	M	47	209	84	1,215	1,319	144	81	118	214	3,431
	F	61	214	153	2,016	1,307	172	36	26	204	4,189
	T	108	423	237	3,231	2,626	316	117	144	418	7,620

1. In Homes for Adults and Homes for Adults and Children.

SOURCE: Canada, Dominion Bureau of Statistics 1944, 678–79 (Statistics Canada; reproduced with permission of the Minister of Supply and Services Canada).

food, shelter and minimal nursing care, while services such as physical or occupational therapy, a dietician or medical supervision were often not available. Nevertheless the costs of prolonged care were often more than many people could afford. In the early decades of this century the cost of health care services were generally the responsibility of the individual. Although insurance schemes were available for the employed, the fit and the young, group plans did not insure the unemployed, the chronically sick and the aged.

1.2.9 Growth of Long-Term Institutional Care Since the 1940s

There was considerable expansion of institutional long-term care after the Second World War, although this varied across the country since responsibility for medical services rests mainly with each province (see also Section 2.2). Following thirty years of various efforts towards health insurance by individual provinces and the federal government, the first provincial hospitalization plan which was universal and compulsory was instituted by Saskatchewan in 1946. A number of other provinces followed and, in 1957, the federal Hospital Insurance and Diagnostic Services Act was passed which provided federal financial assistance to the provinces for health insurance programs through cost-sharing agreements (Gelber 1980, 156–63). Under these programs, the provinces were required to provide inpatient hospital services and this included coverage of chronic and convalescent care. The program commenced in 1958 with British Columbia, Alberta, Saskatchewan, Manitoba, and Newfoundland. These were followed by programs in Ontario, Nova Scotia, New Brunswick and Prince Edward Island in 1959. By the beginning of 1961 residents of all the provinces and territories were covered for hospital and diagnostic services. This eased the cost to individuals of chronic care and, by 1969, there were more than 15,500 beds in 116 chronic care, rehabilitative and convalescent hospitals. These of course were not limited to elderly patients, but they formed a large proportion of the residents (see Chapter 2).

By 1964, *The Canada Year Book 1963–64* (Canada, Dominion Bureau of Statistics 1964, 306) reported that homes for the aged and infirm were provided in all provinces under provincial, municipal or voluntary auspices. Most provinces contributed to the maintenance of elderly persons in homes for the aged, either through general assistance or through statutes that related to these homes. In addition, several provinces and Canada Mortgage and Housing Corporation made capital grants towards the construction of such institutions. In Ontario, for example, The Homes for the Aged Act of 1949 made it mandatory for municipalities to provide and operate homes for the aged, with the province paying half of the capital cost and a portion of the operating costs. Private charitable organizations in Ontario were encouraged by the 1950 amendments to The Charitable Institutions

Act, which provided a provincial subsidy of one thousand dollars per bed for the construction of new buildings for the care of the aged. Additional incentives for municipalities and charitable organizations to upgrade and construct facilities for the aged were provided by legislation passed between 1956 and 1958. In the twenty years from 1949 to 1969 there was a four-fold increase in the number of beds in municipal homes (Ontario Secretariat for Social Development 1981, 29).

A similar expansion occurred in Saskatchewan where, in 1946, the first large nursing home was built in Regina. By 1951 there were twenty-six facilities providing care for the elderly. Eight of these facilities were classified in a report as nursing homes with a total capacity of 631 beds, while the remaining institutions were homes for the aged, which had a total of 478 places and admitted only ambulatory residents (Stolee et al. 1981, 6–12). The report also noted that over 350 persons were being accommodated as long-stay cases in general hospitals. In addition, a large proportion of the institutionalized elderly were accommodated in the province's mental hospitals, due to a combination of insured hospital care for mental illness, a rapid increase in the elderly population in the 1950s, and lack of alternative accommodation. Later, in 1961, a policy of deinstitutionalization of mental hospital patients was accompanied by an increase in the number of elderly residents in nursing homes. By 1963, 2.8% (2,339) of the elderly population was being cared for in mental hospitals, tuberculosis sanitoria, geriatric centres and nursing homes, while approximately 2,000 other people were in "sheltered accommodation." Further development of long-term care institutions in Saskatchewan occurred during the late 1960s and 1970s.

Meanwhile, through the Canada Assistance Plan (CAP), which became effective in 1966, the federal government shared in paying the costs for a variety of residential programs designed for persons in need, or in danger of being in need. These included old age homes. Not only residential facilities for the elderly, but also home-support/homemaking programs were developed by provinces with help from CAP. Later, the Extended Care block grant, instituted under the 1977 Established Programs Financing, replaced certain aspects of CAP, and federal assistance became available for most nursing home care and home health care. Ontario and Manitoba had already begun universal insurance programs for nursing home care and British Columbia began its program with the commencement of the Extended Care block grant. By the early 1980s all but the four Atlantic Provinces had such insurance (Kane and Kane 1985a, 55–56, 60).

In addition to these financial incentives to expansion, legislation passed in Ontario involved many new approaches. The Homes for the Aged Act in 1947 replaced the term "inmate" by "resident." Major changes were introduced by the 1949 Act. Persons could no longer be committed except by a magistrate, and only when the person was at least sixty years of age and the commitment was judged to be in his or her best interests. Residents of a home could not be required to work, although they were encouraged to do so, and handicrafts and similar activities were to be provided. Homes were also required to provide adequate medical services, and identification of residents according to the level of care was also instituted, with nursing supervision for those requiring bed and medical care (Passmore 1967).

Privately run nursing homes in Ontario were brought under the control of the provincial Ministry of Health in 1966 through the Nursing Homes Act, which established operating standards for the approximately five hundred nursing homes then in existence (Ontario Secretariat for Social Development 1981, 29). A new Nursing Homes Act in 1972 provided more detailed operating standards for licensed nursing homes, and an "extended care" benefit was introduced (see Section 2.7). In order to maintain its licence, a nursing home had to provide at least 75% of residents with extended care (Ontario Secretariat for Social Development 1981, 30). As in the chronic care hospitals, the majority of the residents of nursing homes are elderly.

One difficulty associated with determining the number of people in long-term care institutions is the variation in names used for such facilities, both across the provinces and over the years (see also Chapter 3). In Saskatchewan, for example, any institution of less than ten beds providing care for general illness or obstetrics used to be referred to as a nursing home, while a facility with ten or more beds was called a hospital (Stolee et al. 1981, 6). This was changed in 1946 so that the term nursing home was defined to mean an institution where basic nursing care, under medical supervision, was provided to those who required health services beyond just personal care. Names and classification of the care provided were changed again in 1951 and 1958, when certain provincially owned and operated nursing homes were renamed geriatric centres, but often referred to as long-term care hospitals. Other terminology also varies from province to province (see Table 2.1).

Since the 1950s most provinces have instituted systems of classifying different levels of long-term care (e.g., Stolee et al. 1981, 11–14), and set standards for staffing and services. To overcome difficulties caused by differences in provincial classification systems and to clarify health policy, five levels of institutional care were defined in guidelines issued by the federal government in 1973 (see Section 2.2). Additional levels of care within the categories of residential and extended care have been defined by some provinces such as Manitoba and British Columbia (Kane and Kane 1985a, 60; see also Section 2.3). In some cases charges to residents vary with the level of care (see Lang and Shelton 1982, 64–75), and this may have the effect of directing some individuals to a greater level of care than necessary because of lower charges (see also Section 2.8). Because of this issue Saskatchewan, in 1981, established a basic monthly charge for Levels II, III and IV. Level I, which provides supervisory care only, for up to twenty minutes a day, is not subsidized (Stolee et al. 1981, 15).

Mechanisms for admission to long-term institutional care vary across the country. In some areas direct application to the facility of choice is made by the elderly individual or relatives. Elsewhere, application is made to a local "placement coordination service" which matches the individual's needs and abilities to the most appropriate facility with an available bed. In Manitoba and British Columbia, admission is through a single system which includes assessment for both community-based and institutional long-term care (see also Section 2.9).

1.3 SUMMARY AND CONCLUSIONS

This chapter defines long-term institutional care and outlines some of the difficulties in arriving at an appropriate definition (Section 1.1). Section 1.2 traces the history of institutional care in Canada, noting the influence of French and English systems of welfare, and the gradual development of custodial institutions for the destitute of all types and ages, into facilities specifically for the long-term care of the elderly.

Long-term institutional care for the elderly in Canada has changed from being merely part of the limited and reluctant provision for the destitute of all ages to the extensive and varied levels of care available across the country in the 1980s (see Chapter 2). Welfare was originally provided only by private and church philanthropy, but the nineteenth century saw the gradual involvement of government bodies through legislation, financial support and inspection. Recognition of the different needs of those receiving assistance, including the special problems of the elderly, was followed by the establishment of more specialized facilities and classification of levels of care. The increase in the proportion of the elderly, particularly the very old, in the population and financial incentives provided by government legislation, have led to a considerable expansion in long-term care facilities since the Second World War. These facilities are provided under various auspices (see Chapter 2) but with a large component of government support. As a result of such financial assistance, expansion of institutional facilities has been emphasized over the development of community support services, although this is changing (see Chapter 4). Provincial responsibility for health care has resulted in considerable interprovincial variation in services, despite the federal cost-sharing arrangements.

The following may be concluded:

1. It is not easy to arrive at a satisfactory definition of institutional care. The use of various names and different classifications of care confuse the issue, while certain residential settings, such as sheltered housing, occupy a borderline between community and institution.

2. The development of institutional care for the elderly in Canada was affected by the prevailing attitude in the eighteenth and nineteenth centuries that those in need of assistance were largely to blame for their situation. This resulted not only in the bleak and custodial nature of early institutions but also in the reluctance of government bodies to accept responsibility for the care of the elderly. Organization of institutional care varied from province to province. Eventual recognition of governmental responsibility for the urban poor was followed by recognition of the special problems and needs of the elderly.
3. Development of institutions specifically for the aged occurred gradually. Later, considerable expansion was stimulated, not only by the growth in the number of elderly, but also by federal financial assistance to the provinces and various provincial legislation. This encouraged institutional development while neglecting community support services.
4. Interprovincial variation in services remains, as health care is the responsibility of each province.
5. In recent years, there has been some rationalization of the relatively unco-ordinated development of institutional care, and improvement in the quality of care.

NOTE

1. The English counterparts have been chillingly described by Townsend (1962) in *The Last Refuge*.

CHAPTER 2

THE ORGANIZATION OF
INSTITUTIONAL LONG-TERM CARE

2.1 INTRODUCTION

In this chapter, the federal and provincial roles in providing institutional long-term care in Canada will be described briefly, and information will be presented on the types of facilities available, their number and size, the type of resident for whom they provide care, their auspices and funding, and costs to residents.

Most of the statistical data presented for the whole of Canada and for each province were obtained from publications of Statistics Canada. Additional information on federal and provincial roles, and on institutional long-term care in Ontario, Manitoba, and British Columbia, was obtained from a recent valuable review by two United States scholars (Kane and Kane 1985a). That book focusses on the three provinces because their residents have a non-means-tested entitlement to long-term care in nursing homes and, in British Columbia and Manitoba (as also in Ontario to a lesser extent) long-term care services at home are provided by government agencies. It may be noted that Quebec was not included in the discussion by Kane and Kane because of the newness of the program and because of what were considered unique political and cultural factors, nor were the four Atlantic Provinces included since, at the time the book was written, those provinces had not yet provided nursing home care as a universal benefit. Alberta and Saskatchewan were not discussed because they were considered slower in developing home care services than Manitoba and British Columbia (pp. 15–18).

A few other sources were identified that gave information on a national scale. However, the present authors are all based in Ontario, and tended to utilize material that had been sent to them by Ontario organizations, by personal contacts in Ontario, and findings from their own research projects.

2.2 FEDERAL AND PROVINCIAL ROLES

As Kane and Kane point out (1985a, 15, 35), health care in Canada is a provincial responsibility, with each province running its own health care programs. Provinces can use federal cost-sharing by meeting certain general conditions in regard to the comprehensiveness and universality of their programs, their portability across provinces, and the requirement that they be administered publicly on a non-profit basis. The federal government pays about half the actual program costs, using an equalizing formula that gives greater funding to poorer provinces. Otherwise, the provincial governments make their own decisions about the nature of the benefits and the organization of the services. The federal cost-sharing aspects are spelled out in the following items of legislation: (a) the Hospital Insurance and Diagnostic Services Act of 1957 and (b) the Medical Care Act of 1966, which together provide the basis for universal health insurance in Canada; (c) the Federal-Provincial Fiscal Arrangements and Established Programs Act of 1977, which made substantial changes in the cost-sharing arrangements, and (d) the Health Act of 1983, which clarifies and makes the conditions for federal cost-sharing in provincial health programs more stringent.

In addition: (1) the Canada Assistance Plan, introduced in 1966, included financial help to the provinces for health services beyond universal benefits (e.g., care in homes for the aged and nursing homes, clothing and comfort allowances in institutions); (2) the Extended Health Care Services Program, introduced by the federal government in 1977, assists the provinces in providing less expensive alternatives to hospitalization, including extended care, residential care, home care, and ambulatory care (see also Section 1.2.9).

Kane and Kane also point out that (1985a, 60):

> To clarify health policy, the federal government issued guidelines in 1973, setting forth and defining five levels of institutional care:
>
> 1. Residential
> 2. Extended Care
> 3. Chronic hospital
> 4. Rehabilitation
> 5. Acute hospital.
>
> Care at levels 3 through 5 is automatically covered by provincial health insurance programs. All provinces further differentiate an extended care level (analogous to nursing homes) and a residential care level for persons needing minimal health care. Not all provinces with insured nursing home benefits reach down to level 1: Manitoba and British Columbia do; Ontario does not.

The "chronic hospital" level is often referred to as "chronic care," and the "rehabilitation" level includes "special rehabilitation."

2.3 LEVELS OF INSTITUTIONAL LONG-TERM CARE

All long-term care provided by institutions can be thought of as being provided at one of three levels – residential care, extended care, or chronic care.

Illustrative of provincial definitions of these levels of care are the following from the Ontario Ministry of Health (1980, 3):
Residential care is defined as:

> that required by a person who is ambulant and/or independently mobile, who has decreased physical and/or mental faculties, and who requires primarily supervision and/or assistance with activities of daily living and provision for meeting psychosocial needs through social and recreational services. The period of time during which care is required is indeterminate and related to the individual condition.

Extended care is defined as:

> Care required by a person with a relatively stabilized (physical or mental) chronic desease or functional disability, who having reached the apparent limit of his recovery, is not likely to change in the near future, who has relatively little need for the diagnostic and therapeutic services of a hospital but who requires availability of personal care on a continuing 24-hr. basis with medical and professional nursing supervision and provision for meeting psychosocial needs. The period of time during which care is required is unpredictable but usually consists of a matter of months or years.

Chronic care is defined as:

> Care required by a person who is chronically ill and/or has a functional disability (physical or mental) whose acute phase of illness is over, whose vital processes may or may not be stable, whose potential for rehabilitation may be limited, and who requires a range of therapeutic services, medical management and skilled nursing care plus provision for meeting psychosocial needs. The period of time during which care is required is unpredictable but usually consists of a matter of months or years.

A somewhat different approach is illustrated by the following definitions of four levels of long-term care in Manitoba (Kane and Kane 1985a, 109):

> Level 1. Indicates minimal dependence on nursing time. The individual requires weekly supervision and/or assistance with personal care and/or some encouragement or reminders to wash, dress, and attend meals and/or activities. He/she may need administration of medications on a regular basis and to use mechanical aids.
>
> Level 2. Indicates moderate dependence on nursing time for at least one of the following categories: bathing and dressing, feeding, treatments, ambulation, elimination, and/or support and/or supervision.
>
> Level 3. Indicates maximum dependence on nursing time for two or three of the following categories: bathing and dressing, feeding, treatments, ambulation, elimination, and/or support and/or supervision or maximum dependence for support and/or supervision and moderate dependence for at least two of the other categories.
>
> Level 4. Indicates maximum dependence on nursing time for four or more of the following categories: bathing and dressing, feeding, treatment, ambulation, elimination, and support and/or supervision.

The levels of care translate into staffing guidelines for care provided by long-term care institutions as follows:

> Level 1 – 0.5 total paid hours of nursing care per resident day (10 percent Registered Nurse (RN) and 90 percent nursing assistant).
>
> Level 2 – 2.0 total paid hours of nursing care per resident day (10 percent RN, 30 percent Licensed Practical Nurse (LPN), and 70 percent nursing assistant).
>
> Levels 3 and 4 – 3.5 total paid hours of nursing care per resident day (20 percent RN, 15 percent LPN, and 65 percent nursing assistant).

In British Columbia, five levels of long-term care are defined, as follows (Kane and Kane 1985a, 144):

> Personal Care. Persons at this level are independently mobile with or without mechanical aids, mentally intact, or suffering only minor mental impairment. They may require a protected housing environment, social stimulation, or minor assistance with self-care, but do not need regular medical supervision. A personal care facility offers 24-hours-a-day supervison by non-professional personnel, a protective environment, help with activities of daily living, and a social/recreational program.
>
> Intermediate Care 1 (IC–1). Persons at this level are independently mobile, similar to those requiring personal care, but will need some health supervision and some assistance with activities of daily living as well as the protected environment and social/recreational program already mentioned. It is estimated that a person at this level in institutional care would need 75 minutes of individual attention per day – 15 minutes from a professional and 60 minutes from a non-professional.
>
> Intermediate Care 2 (IC–2). The client's characteristics resemble those above, but the estimated amount of care needed for such clients in facilities is increased to 100 minutes of daily individual attention – 30 minutes by a professional and 70 minutes by a non-professional.
>
> Intermediate Care 3 (IC–3). This level of care was designed to recognize the psychogeriatric client with severe, continuous behavioural problems. The level is also used for persons needing more daily care than allowed under IC–2, especially those awaiting room in an Extended Care hospital. The assumption for care in this category is 120 minutes of individual care daily – 30 minutes from a professional and 90 minutes from a non-professional.
>
> Extended Care. An extended care hospital unit provides round-the-clock supervision of a registered nurse and the availability of regular medical supervision and a multi-disciplinary therapeutic team. It is assumed the individual will need at least 150 minutes of care a day. The rule-of-thumb for eligibility is that this individual generally is unable to transfer independently.

2.4 TYPES OF LONG-TERM CARE INSTITUTIONAL FACILITIES

There is no simple correspondence between the level of long-term care and the designation of the facility. The same level of care is provided by facilities with different names in different provinces. Even within a province, the same level of care can be provided by facilities that have different names, and a given facility can provide more than one level of care.

Some of this variability is illustrated in Table 2.1. Kane and Kane (1985a) note that Manitoba uses the term "Personal Care Home" to refer to the entire institutional program, whereas British Columbia uses the term "Personal Care" to refer to the lowest level of institutional care. The term "Extended Care" in Ontario refers to care received by people eligible for the extended health benefit, because they require more than one and a half hours of nursing care per day. They may reside in either homes for the aged or in nursing homes. However, Manitoba and British Columbia use the term "Extended Care" to refer to a relatively heavy level of care; these extended care units are usually found in hospitals and correspond to chronic care hospitals in Ontario, which may be either freestanding or be attached to acute care hospitals. In British Columbia, the term "Private Hospital" refers to for-profit nursing homes which house patients requiring the heaviest care level (p. 61).

Canadian Pensioners Concerned has published a directory which gives brief descriptions of categories of long-term care facilities available in each province (Lang and Shelton 1982, 63–75). With respect to provinces other than the three previously referred to in this section, the directory suggests the following: (1) facilities that provide long-term care at the residential care level appear to be available in all of the other provinces. They are called Special Care Homes in New Brunswick, Newfoundland, and Saskatchewan; Licensed Boarding Homes and Homes for the Aged in Nova Scotia; Manors in Prince Edward Island; Pavillons in Quebec; and Senior Citizens Lodges in Alberta; (2) all of the other provinces appear to have facilities that provide long-term care at the Extended Care Level. They are called Nursing Homes in Alberta, New Brunswick, Newfoundland, Nova Scotia, and Prince Edward Island; Special Care Homes in Saskatchewan; and Reception Centres in Quebec.

2.5 DATA ON SPECIAL CARE FACILITIES

Special Care Facilities are defined by Statistics Canada (1984a) as "Residential special care facilities with four or more beds for residents other than staff and which provide care to at least one resident." They are, in general, "maintained for people, chronically ill or disabled, who reside there more or less permanently." Hospitals are excluded from the category of special care facilities; the latter are thus mainly those that provide residential and extended care as defined in Section 2.3 and illustrated in Table 2.1, although they would also appear to include the Personal Care Homes, Level 4 in Manitoba which provide chronic care.

Statistics Canada reports (1984a) that there were 2,450 special care facilities in Canada in 1983 for which the "principal characteristic of the predominant group of residents" was "aged person."[1] These 2,450 special care facilities had 159,514 beds, or an average of 65 beds per facility, and this represents a rate of 67.6 such beds per 1,000 population over age sixty-five, using the 1981 census figure as the denominator (Statistics Canada 1982).

TABLE 2.1

FACILITIES IN MANITOBA, BRITISH COLUMBIA, AND ONTARIO THAT PROVIDE DIFFERENT LEVELS OF LONG-TERM CARE

Level of Care	Manitoba[1]	British Columbia[2]	Ontario[3]
Level 1 (Residential)	Personal Care Home, Level 1 (Hostels)	Personal Care Boarding Homes	Homes for the Aged Rest/Boarding Homes
Level 2 (Extended)	Personal Care Home, Level 2	Intermediate Care, 1–IC1	Homes for the Aged
	Personal Care Home, Level 3	Intermediate Care, 2–IC2	(Extended Care)
		Intermediate Care, 3–IC3	Nursing Homes Satellite Homes
Level 3 (Chronic)	Personal Care Home, Level 4 Extended Care Units	Extended Care Units Private Hospitals	Chronic Hospitals

1. All 4 levels are part of Personal Care Home Program of the Manitoba Health Services Commission.
2. Access to all 5 levels is controlled by the Long-Term Care Program, which monitors care in the lower 4 levels. Extended Care standards are still part of the Hospital Program.
3. The Homes for the Aged Program is administered by the Ontario Department of Community and Social Services; the Nursing Home and Chronic Hospital Programs are administered by the Instutional Services Program in the Ontario Department of Health.

SOURCE: Kane and Kane 1985a, p. 62.

The type of auspice or ownership of these 2,450 facilities is shown in Table 2.2. For Canada as a whole, more of the beds were in Proprietary facilities (37.0%) than in any other type, with Municipal, Public Undistributed, and Lay being the next most important types of auspice. "Public Undistributed" is a designation used only in the province of Quebec. In Ontario, the designation "Charitable" is used to include both lay and religious auspices. The major types of auspices for these special care facilities varied considerably between provinces (Table 2.3). In most provinces proprietary and/or municipal facilities were the most common but, while more than half of Ontario's beds for elderly people in special care facilities are proprietary, this proportion is only 27% in the rest of Canada. The reasons for this difference are not obvious but are presumably partly historical.

The overall rate of provision of beds in special care facilities in 1983 per 1,000 population aged 65 and older varied from a low of 57.4 in Quebec to a high of 91.2 in Alberta (Table 2.3). There was no consistent geographic pattern, as Nova Scotia had the second lowest rate (62.0) followed closely by British Columbia (62.2), while New Brunswick had the second highest rate (75.0).

TABLE 2.2

**NUMBER OF SPECIAL CARE FACILITIES PREDOMINANTLY FOR AGED
PERSONS, AND BEDS IN THESE FACILITIES, BY TYPE OF AUSPICE,
CANADA, 1983**

Auspices	No. of Facilities	Beds	Per Cent of Total Beds
Proprietary[1]	1,118	59,024	37.0
Municipal	348	33,137	20.8
Public Undistributed[2]	482	25,608	16.1
Lay[3]	280	22,606	14.2
Religious	156	14,394	9.0
Provincial	63	4,512	2.8
Federal	3	233	0.1
Total[4]	2,450	159,514	100.0

1. Private individual, partnership, or corporation, and run for profit.
2. Used only in Quebec.
3. Non-profit voluntary associations, societies or fraternities.
4. This corresponds to an average of 65 beds per facility.

SOURCE: Statistics Canada 1984a. Reproduced with permission of the Minister of Supply and Services Canada.

2.6 INSTITUTIONAL CARE AT THE RESIDENTIAL CARE LEVEL: ILLUSTRATIONS FROM ONTARIO

The Ontario Ministry of Health's definition of long-term care at the residential care level was given in Section 2.3. This source also indicated that such care is provided in "a residential setting," including "an individual's own home (private family living)," certain congregate living facilities such as "foster homes" or "boarding homes" which are not usually perceived as institutions, and settings such as residential care homes (e.g., rest homes, retirement homes), homes for the aged, and nursing homes.

In Ontario, while an elderly person needing institutional care at the residential care level could obtain it in a nursing home, he/she would not be likely to do so, because nursing homes generally charge more than residential care homes or homes for the aged, and the province does not pay any part of the client's residential care charges. Thus, in Ontario, the latter types of facility provide the majority of institutional residential care.

Information from the Long-Term Residential Care Association of Ontario (personal communication 1985) indicates that residential care homes provide food and lodging, recreation and social activities, personal care, and light nursing care when needed. They will not admit an individual who requires more than one and a half hours per day of nursing care, and unlike

TABLE 2.3

NUMBER OF SPECIAL CARE FACILITIES PREDOMINANTLY FOR AGED PERSONS, AND BEDS IN THESE FACILITIES, FOR MAJOR TYPES OF AUSPICES IN EACH PROVINCE, 1983[1]

Province[2]	Auspices	No. of Facilities	Beds	Beds per 1,000 Population Aged 65 + [3]
Newfoundland	Religious	15	1,349	
	Proprietary	56	994	
	Total (all auspices)	78	3,093	70.3
Prince Edward Island	Provincial	6	496	
	Proprietary	16	284	
	Total (all auspices)	24	977	65.6
Nova Scotia	Proprietary	64	2,370	
	Municipal	23	1,931	
	Total (all auspices)	100	5,707	62.0
New Brunswick	Lay	46	2,752	
	Proprietary	120	1,407	
	Total (all auspices)	179	5,349	75.0
Quebec	Public Undistributed	482	25,608	
	Proprietary	155	7,092	
	Total (all auspices)	637	32,700	57.4
Ontario	Proprietary	434	32,602	
	Municipal	92	18,555	
	Lay	58	5,236	
	Total (all auspices)	628	61,237	70.5
Manitoba	Lay	41	2,700	
	Proprietary	35	2,603	
	Religious	22	2,039	
	Total (all auspices)	126	8,305	68.1
Saskatchewan	Municipal	84	4,081	
	Religious	29	1,999	
	Total (all auspices)	135	8,574	73.9
Alberta	Municipal	119	7,421	
	Proprietary	36	3,606	
	Provincial	41	2,078	
	Total (all auspices)	218	14,966	91.2
British Columbia	Lay	107	9,554	
	Proprietary	195	7,332	
	Total (all auspices)	321	18,533	62.2

1. Only the two or three major specific types of auspices with respect to number of beds are shown for each province.
2. The Northwest Territories had 2 such facilities with 12 beds, and the Yukon Territory had 2 with 61 beds. These beds account for the difference between Tables 2.2 and 2.3 in the total number of beds in Canada.
3. Using 1981 census figures as denominators (Statistics Canada 1982).

SOURCE: Statistics Canada 1984a. Reproduced with permission of the Minister of Supply and Services Canada.

the homes for the aged, they usually transfer a resident requiring this level of care to another appropriate facility. Residential care homes try to emphasize good nutrition, activation, and control over the administration of prescribed drugs. The great majority of their residents are elderly, although some of these facilities also have some mentally retarded residents and/or "Homes for Special Care" residents (persons discharged from psychiatric hospitals) of all ages.

Almost all residential care homes in Ontario are commercial enterprises, privately owned and operated. This is also true of nursing homes. Residential and nursing care homes are the two types of special care facilities included under proprietary auspices in Tables 2.2 and 2.3. However, unlike nursing homes, residential care homes are not covered by any provincial legislation in Ontario, nor are they under the jurisdiction of any provincial ministry; they are under the supervision of the Medical Officer of Health of each District or County Health Unit, and are usually covered by municipal legislation. This municipal legislation usually involves fire, safety and physical accommodation standards only, but not standards regarding staffing or the care provided. Such lack of enforceable standards of care, combined with the lack of provincial government regulation or supervision of the operation of these residential care homes, is considered to be one of the current major problems in the system of long-term institutional care of the elderly in Ontario. The Government of Ontario is now considering taking steps to remedy the situation through appropriate legislation (Van Horne 1986, 19).

There is substantial variation between different residential care homes in their size and daily charges, with the most expensive ones catering to affluent elderly people and charging about one hundred dollars per day. However, the daily charge to residents in residential care homes in Ontario averages about thirty dollars (personal communication, Long-Term Residential Care Association of Ontario 1985). Since residential care homes are not under the jurisdiction of the provincial government in Ontario, precise information on the number of such facilities in the province is not available.[2]

Homes for the aged in Ontario provide at least a place of residence, meals, services such as laundry, access to a physician-in-charge, and social and recreational opportunities, to primarily elderly residents. If that is all that a resident requires, he or she will be accommodated at the residential care level (also called the normal care level). The resident may also receive some personal care in carrying out the activities of daily living, and/or up to one and a half hours of nursing care per day, if needed. Other professional services such as chiropodist, physio and occupational therapists and social workers may be available.

The majority of homes for the aged in Ontario also provide care at the extended care (or bed care) level, to residents who require more than one and a half hours of personal and/or nursing care per day (see Section 2.7.1).

Some homes for the aged also have a special care level, wing or unit, which is a physically separate and sometimes locked area, for residents with advanced organic brain disease. Residents with milder degrees of dementia may be living among the other residents in the other two levels of care, but if the condition worsens so that the special staffing and/or physical arrangements in the special care unit are required, the resident will be transferred.

Homes for the aged in Ontario are under the auspices of either a municipality or a charitable organization. The Ontario Ministry of Community and Social Services has jurisdiction over the homes for the aged through the Homes for the Aged Acts of 1947 and 1949, and subsequent amendments (Ontario Secretariat for Social Development 1981, 29). The Ministry pays half of the capital cost, and an average of about half of the operating costs of each home for the aged (based on a formula applied individually to each home). The remaining costs are covered by the municipality or charitable organization under whose auspices the home operates, and by charges paid by residents.

In Ontario, anyone over age sixty is automatically eligible for admission to a municipal home for the aged. Younger individuals may obtain approval for admission if their needs require the care available, and in the judgement of the home administrator there is no other feasible arrangement or facility nearby to meet those needs. In practice, the municipal homes for the aged have a small number of residents in their forties and a few more in their fifties, but the average age of their residents is approximately eighty-four years. The homes for the aged under charitable auspices do not have to get approval to admit someone under age sixty, but function similarly to the municipal facilities in this respect, and have only a slightly higher proportion of residents who are under age sixty (personal communication, R. Fleming, Ontario Ministry of Community and Social Services 1985).

The charge per day for residential care ward accommodation in a home for the aged varies between homes, but generally exceeds thirty dollars in Ontario (personal communication, R. Fleming). If the resident is unable to pay all of this, the province will provide some financial assistance but the resident has to pay at least $18.75 a day. Assistance is calculated on the basis of income from Old Age Security/Guaranteed Income Supplement, but leaving $112 per month for the resident's personal use. It should be noted that this differs from the financial arrangements for residential care in nursing homes and residential homes where no such assistance is available. Most municipal homes for the aged do not charge different rates for private, semi-private, or ward accommodation, but instead use these different accommodation arrangements according to how well residents are able to mix with others. The charitable homes for the aged, however, charge more for private and usually for semi-private accommodation.

As mentioned in Section 1.2.9, after passage of the Homes for the Aged Act in Ontario in 1949, there was a rapid growth in bed capacity in homes for the aged in that province. For example, bed capacity in municipal homes for the aged rose from about 3,700 beds in 1949 to about 15,000 beds in 1969 (Ontario Secretariat for Social Development 1981, 29). At present, there are about 28,000 beds in all homes for the aged in Ontario, of which more than 18,000 are in the ninety-one municipal homes and a little less than 10,000 in the ninety charitable homes (personal communication, R. Fleming 1985). Of those in charitable homes, more than half are in homes under lay auspices, and the remainder are in homes under religious auspices (Statistics Canada 1984a). About 17,000 of all beds in homes for the aged in Ontario are at the residential care level and 11,000 at the extended care level. The homes for the aged built in the twenty-year period following passage of the Homes for the Aged Act have the vast majority of their beds in four-bed rooms. For example, the municipal home in Kingston, which has a total of 231 beds, has 180 beds in four-bed rooms, 38 in two-bed rooms, and 13 in one-bed rooms. The homes for the aged built after 1970 have almost all two-bed rooms, and those being built now have an increasing proportion of one-bed rooms. This change is due to more recent concerns about the privacy and quality of life of the residents (personal communication, R. Fleming 1985).

Some information on facilities, in provinces other than Ontario, that provide long-term care at the residential care level, was given in Section 2.4. In those other provinces, the auspices of such facilities are a mix of both proprietary and non-proprietary and, unlike Ontario, such facilities in other provinces are subject to provincial legislation and regulation (Kane and Kane 1985a, 111, 115, 163; Lang and Shelton 1982, 64–75).

2.7 INSTITUTIONAL CARE AT THE EXTENDED CARE LEVEL: ILLUSTRATIONS FROM ONTARIO

As explained in Section 2.3, different terminology is used for the levels of care provided in each province. In Ontario, for example, long-term care at the extended care level is available in homes for the aged and in nursing homes, and this will be discussed in turn.

2.7.1 Homes for the Aged

A resident is normally admitted to a home for the aged in Ontario at the residential care level but can be transferred to the extended care level if he or she develops the need for at least one and a half hours of skilled nursing care per day. An application for extended care must be completed and signed by the applicant's physician, and be approved by the Extended Care Division of the Ontario Ministry of Health. If a resident has been approved for extended care and has been transferred to an extended care bed, he or she currently only has to pay $20.44 per day (as of Feb. 1, 1987); the remaining costs are paid by the Ontario Health Insurance Plan (OHIP).

Each home for the aged in Ontario is currently restricted regarding the proportion of its total beds that can be at the extended care level, according to a formula that averages out to approximately 40% of its total beds. This is proving to be inadequate because increasing longevity among residents is associated with a need for heavier care. In addition, because applications to homes for the aged come from an older population, fewer admissions occur at the residential care level, and there is pressure for admissions at the extended care level. This trend is probably because of the spread of chronic home-care programs and expansion of other community living arrangements and support services. The restrictions imposed by the province on the expansion of nursing home beds led to homes for the aged being given extended care beds to compensate them for the cost of maintaining people who require more than one and a half hours of nursing care per day. As a result, homes for the aged are becoming increasingly similar to nursing homes. Furthermore, there is now pressure to allow admissions to a home for the aged at the extended care level and to increase the proportion of total beds in each home which can be at the extended care level.

2.7.2 Nursing Homes

The majority of residents in nursing homes in Ontario are elderly persons receiving care at the extended care level. There used to be a relatively small number of nursing home beds approved by the Ontario Ministry of Health for care at the chronic care level, but these approvals have almost all been phased out. Many nursing homes in Ontario are also licensed as homes for special care for people of all ages discharged from provincial mental retardation or psychiatric facilities.

In Ontario, many nursing homes are proprietary institutions run for profit by their owners. In contrast, data reported for two other provinces (Kane and Kane 1985b) show that in Manitoba only 29% of nursing home beds were in proprietary facilities and 37% in British Columbia (see Table 2.3). Most proprietary nursing home owners own and operate one or sometimes two nursing homes, but there are a few corporations, such as Extendicare, that own and operate a chain of homes. Nursing homes in Ontario were brought under control of the Ontario Ministry of Health by the Nursing Home Act of 1966, which established operating standards (Ontario Secretariat for Social Development 1981, 29). These standards were further spelled out in the Nursing Home Act of 1972. Similar legislation has been passed in other provinces, for example in British Columbia. The standards are detailed and broad in scope, covering physical aspects such as square footage requirements in bedrooms and bathrooms, staffing requirements, nutritional standards for the meals served to residents, and other aspects of the care provided to residents. The Ontario Ministry of Health licenses and inspects all nursing homes in the province, through its Nursing Homes Branch.

The daily charge in Ontario for residents of nursing homes who are receiving extended care benefits is currently $48.90 for those in standard ward accommodation, $56.08 for those in semi-private ward accommodation, and $63.26 for those in private accommodation. In each case, the Ontario government pays the extended care benefits of $28.46, and the resident is responsible for paying the remainder. As with residents of homes for the aged, the resident co-payment for those in standard ward accommodation is calculated to ensure that residents with no private sources of income, who are receiving the usual amount of government old age social security payments, are left with a disposable income or "comfort allowance" of $112 a month. Information obtained from the administrator of a sixty-six bed, long-established nursing home in the Kingston area, which is probably fairly typical, indicates that 9% of its beds were in private accommodation in one-bed rooms, 36% were in semi-private accommodation in two-bed rooms, and 55% were in standard ward accommodation in rooms with three or more beds (personal communication 1985).

While the number of licensed nursing homes in Ontario declined 26%, from 447 to 332, between 1973 and 1984, the number of licensed nursing home beds increased 30%, from 22,505 to 29,215 (Social Planning Council of Metro Toronto 1984). Thus, the average number of beds per home increased from 50 to 88 during this period. Many smaller, older nursing homes closed during that time, including a number which had failed to pass inspection and to obtain a renewal of their license, but continued to operate as residential care homes with essentially the same facilities, residents, staff, and programs of care, but without the funding assistance provided to nursing homes. Also a number of new, larger nursing homes opened during this period.

When they are proprietary institutions run for profit, nursing homes sometimes present serious problems even though most now seem to be progressive and caring in their approach. While "horror stories" of gross abuse or neglect of residents in a nursing home used to appear in the press, especially in the United States, more often than they do now, such incidents still occur. For financial reasons, nursing homes are reluctant to admit someone who requires a substantial amount of care but does not qualify for care at the chronic care level in a hospital. They may refuse admission to such a person, who is then likely to be admitted to a home for the aged at the residential care level. Care is then provided as well as possible by a staff complement which is inadequate to meet the needs of such residents, until a vacancy occurs at the extended care level. There is currently pressure on the Ontario Ministry of Health to alleviate this problem by recognizing more than one level of care within the extended care level, as in Manitoba and

British Columbia (see Table 2.1), and reimbursing nursing homes at a higher rate for residents who require heavier care.

2.8 INSTITUTIONAL CARE AT THE CHRONIC CARE LEVEL

Virtually all care at this level in Canada (see Section 2.3) is provided in hospitals. As seen in Table 2.4 (Statistics Canada 1985), about 60% of the hospital beds available for chronic care are in hospitals that are called extended care hospitals in some provinces and chronic care hospitals in others. The remaining beds at this level of care are in long-term units of general hospitals. The average number of beds in the extended care (including chronic care) hospitals is 244.

Table 2.4 shows that the rates of such beds per 1,000 population aged 65+ were low in the eastern provinces and in Saskatchewan, moderate in Manitoba and Ontario, high in Alberta and British Columbia, and were highest in Quebec.

TABLE 2.4

NUMBER OF LONG-TERM CARE BEDS AT THE CHRONIC CARE LEVEL, IN EXTENDED CARE (INCLUDING CHRONIC) HOSPITALS, AND IN LONG-TERM UNITS OF GENERAL HOSPITALS, BY PROVINCE, 1982–83

| | Long-Term Care Beds at Chronic Care Level | | | |
| | | | Total Long-Term Care Beds Chronic Care Level | |
Province	In Extended Care Hospitals	In Long-Term Units of General Hospitals[1]	No.	No. per 1,000 Population Aged 65+ [2]
Canada, Total	29,333	20,084	49,417	20.9
Newfoundland	0	159	159	3.6
Prince Edward Island	45	0	45	3.0
Nova Scotia	0	274	274	3.0
New Brunswick	0	438	438	6.1
Quebec	17,165	6,728	23,893	42.0
Ontario	5,532	5,692	11,224	12.9
Manitoba	380	845	1,225	10.0
Saskatchewan	264	255	519	4.5
Alberta	3,621	1,044	4,665	28.6
British Columbia	2,326	4,649	6,975	23.4

1. Excludes beds in rehabilitation units.

2. Using 1981 census figures as denominators (Statistics Canada 1982).

SOURCE: Statistics Canada 1985. Reproduced with permission of the Minister of Supply and Services Canada.

The majority of beds in chronic care hospitals in Ontario are located in large metropolitan centres. In contrast, most chronic care wings in general hospitals are located in smaller centres, to enable patients who live far from a metropolitan centre to receive chronic care while remaining close to their family and community. Chronic care wings in general hospitals tend to provide adequate medical care, but they place less emphasis than chronic care hospitals on rehabilitation therapies. They also provide less in the way of social, recreational, and activational programs, which contribute to the patient's quality of life.

Table 2.5 gives the total number of long-term care beds for each province in 1983 based on the sum of beds in special care facilities in Tables 2.2 and 2.3 as well as those at the chronic care level in hospitals in Table 2.4. The rate of these beds per thousand population aged sixty-five and over is lowest in the three most easterly provinces, moderate in New Brunswick, Ontario, Manitoba, Saskatchewan and British Columbia, high in Quebec, and higher still in Alberta. For Canada as a whole, the number of such beds in special care facilities was about three times greater than the number in hospitals.

TABLE 2.5

NUMBER OF LONG-TERM CARE BEDS, BY PROVINCE, 1983

	Total Long-Term Care Beds[1]	
Province	No.	No. per 1,000 Population Age 65+ [2]
Canada, Total	208,931[3]	88.5
Newfoundland	3,252	73.9
Prince Edward Island	1,022	68.6
Nova Scotia	5,981	65.0
New Brunswick	5,787	81.1
Quebec	56,593	99.4
Ontario	72,461	83.4
Manitoba	9,530	78.1
Saskatchewan	9,093	78.4
Alberta	19,631	120.4
British Columbia	25,508	85.6

1. In special care facilities predominantly for aged persons (Tables 2.2 and 2.3), or at the chronic care level in extended care (including chronic care hospitals or in long-term units of general hospitals (Table 2.4).

2. Using 1981 census figures as denominators (Statistics Canada 1982).

3. Includes 12 beds in Northwest Territories and 61 in Yukon Territory.

SOURCE: Tables 2.2, 2.3 and 2.4.

In Ontario, chronic care hospitals, like general and psychiatric hospitals, are under the jurisdiction of the Ministry of Health. Costs for chronic care are covered primarily by OHIP for basic accommodation, for which the average cost is now $158 per day. However, if the patient is over age eighteen, he or she must pay $20.44 per day for each day of stay after 60 days in a chronic care hospital or chronic care wing of a general hospital, unless the attending physician certifies that the patient is receiving rehabilitation and is expected to return home within 240 days of admission. This is the same charge that a resident would pay in a nursing home if covered by extended care. The rationale behind this patient co-payment provision is to discourage patients from remaining in a chronic care hospital for financial reasons when nursing home accommodation would be adequate. On average, a semi-private bed costs the patient an additional $11 a day, and a private bed $19 a day more than ward accommodation.

Thus in Ontario the resident or patient pays the whole cost of care in residential care, a smaller amount in extended care (because of OHIP's extended care benefit), and nothing during the first sixty days in chronic care. This differential has the undesirable consequence of motivating some patients and their families to seek admission to an unnecessarily intensive level of care for financial reasons. (A similar financial disincentive for improvement used to exist in Saskatchewan until changes were made in 1981; Stolee et al. 1981, 14–15.) This is not only economically costly to society, because total costs are greater at the more intensive level of care, but it is also undesirable for the patient to be in a setting where most other patients are more severely disabled, and where staffing, facilities, and programs of care are geared to more severely disabled patients. This tends to encourage dependency. It would seem preferable to have a system in which the daily charge to the patient was constant (representing the cost of the basic custodial care items of food, shelter, etc., which he or she would have to spend if living in the community), regardless of the level of care provided. In addition to avoiding an inappropriate steering effect on the patient, such a system would be easier to understand and would thus be helpful to physicians and other health care professionals advising the elderly.

2.9 COMPARISONS BETWEEN ONTARIO, MANITOBA AND BRITISH COLUMBIA

Unfortunately, in a book of this size it is not possible to make a comprehensive comparison of information relevant to long-term care in each of the provinces of Canada. Moreover, accurate data are not readily available, since in many provinces changes are taking place in the systems of long-term care, and what may be correct in one year is likely to be out of date in subsequent years. At the same time, it is useful to make some qualitative comparisons to illustrate the substantial differences which exist between various provinces. Kane and Kane's (1985a) impression of the situation in Ontario, Manitoba, and British Columbia is quoted as a summary:

Ontario's long-term care programs are less controlled than those in British Columbia and Manitoba. Allocation of services to those most in need, thus controlling the use of institutional beds, has not been entirely successful, as there is no consistent case management or other such system. Efforts have been made to develop mechanisms to co-ordinate services and to set priorities. For example, various local planning bodies, such as District Health Councils, and Placement Co-ordination Services have been established, which, however, are not able to exercise comprehensive and authoritative control (p. 65).

Manitoba, in contrast to Ontario, has a single point of entry to both community and institutionally based long-term care. This is done through an assessment team which examines the functional need for assistance and decides whether home care or a personal care home is appropriate in light of the client's preference, the social situation and the availability of community services. The program also assesses the competing needs of different persons who are waiting in a particular community. A special feature is that each applicant is reviewed by a panel before being accepted and placed on a waiting list; this avoids a hasty judgement, based on insufficient information (p. 105).

In British Columbia the administration involves twenty-two regional health units which use a case management system. Unlike Manitoba, the case managers in British Columbia are responsible for assessing and authorizing levels of on-going care not only in the home, but also in facilities. Also, a management information system has been established, which can be used to monitor service providers and assist managers to evaluate their client. A standardized assessment tool is used throughout the province. In addition, the case manager completes a relatively simple "Care Advice Form," when a service is started, stopped or changed, which is used to verify payment. It also provides a record, which can be used for statistical purposes, of any change in service that has occurred (pp. 142, 152–55).

British Columbia's program has been developed recently, using the experience of other jurisdictions. Kane and Kane believe that it represents the highest level of co-ordination and formalization. It is noteworthy that the long-term care program is located in the same unit of the Ministry as the hospital program, and that the same assessors determine client needs and control facility placement and reassessment in a relatively structured manner. An information system has been developed within the program, although it is not yet linked to acute care (pp. 169–70).

Both British Columbia and Manitoba have systems whereby a case manager can accept referral from any interested party. A referral is followed by an early assessment, which in turn assigns a level of care, bearing in mind the home situation. Generally, home care is not authorized if it is more expensive than institutional care. The case manager is responsible, together with the service providers, for monitoring the care provided and making reassessments routinely and as needed.

The differences between Manitoba and British Columbia concern the authority of case managers. In Manitoba, the manager is responsible for the procedure which leads to institutional care and for the management of the waiting list, but this responsibility ceases when the client enters the facility. In British Columbia, case managers follow the client whether admission is into a facility or home care. They continue to conduct periodic assessments and can authorize individual services, both in the community and in the institution. However in British Columbia, but not in Manitoba, home nursing and other therapies, such as occupational therapy, etc., are not responsibilites of the long-term case manager (pp. 205–10).

Kane and Kane believe that duplication and lack of co-ordination are most pronounced in Ontario. They note, correctly, that the acute hospital program, the extended care program and portions of the home care programs are operated by separate entities within the Ministry of Health, but other services, including homes for the aged, some homemaking and community long-term care support programs, are operated by the Ministry of Community and Social Services (p. 238).

Kane and Kane are particularly critical of the quality of care in Ontario nursing homes and noted the greatest dissatisfaction there. Specifically, the system of inspection is regarded as too weak, since prior notification allows the home to prepare for it. Moreover, the results of such inspections are not made public, thus making it difficult for a client to choose a home. Also, the voluntary system of accreditation, operated by the Canadian Council on Hospital Accreditation, is believed to be self-serving and provider-dominated. To counter what may be regarded as lobbying efforts by the providers of long-term care, a consumer advocate group, the Concerned Friends of Ontario Citizens in Care Facilities, has been formed. This group prepared a number of highly critical position papers which stress the lack of rehabilitation, privacy, and choice, the unsanitary and unsafe conditions, and inadequate or demeaning social contacts (pp. 247–48).

2.10 SUMMARY AND CONCLUSIONS

This chapter outlines the types of long-term care institutional facilities which exist in Canada and which can be viewed in the light of the historical perspective outlined in Chapter 1. The chapter also indicates the increased specialization of services which has occurred in attempting to meet the different needs of the various groups of the frail elderly. These institutions range from residential care homes in which the relatively well elderly are located, through homes for the aged, and nursing homes to chronic care facilities, where the more severely disabled elderly are housed. The criteria and funding of these various institutions are discussed.

The following may be concluded:

1. The provision of institutional long-term care for the frail elderly varies significantly between the different provinces, although federal cost-sharing regulations require that certain conditions regarding the comprehensiveness and universality of their programs be met.
2. In particular, the co-ordination of services at different levels of care varies considerably from province to province.
3. In some provinces, the charges for the different types of institutions are not the same and frequently such charges are less in institutions providing more intensive care. This may tend to steer elderly clients to inappropriate placement in institutions providing more extensive care. Such economic steering effects could be avoided if the daily charge to a patient was the same regardless of the level of care provided.

NOTES

1. In other special care facilities the principal characteristics of the predominant group of residents include "physical handicap, retarded, mental handicap, emotionally disturbed children, alcohol/drug, delinquent, transient, and other."
2. The owners of approximately 200 residential care homes involving about 7,000 beds are members of the Long-Term Residential Care Association of Ontario. This Association does not have accurate information regarding the number of beds in residential care homes belonging to owners who are not members of the Association. However, while it is therefore not possible to make a good estimate from the available data, the Association believes that there are a total of about 450 residential care homes in Ontario involving about 18,000 beds; a minimal estimate is 300 such homes with about 10,000 beds. This estimate for Ontario seems far too high, in view of the known number of 182 homes for the aged involving about 28,000 beds (personal communication, R. Fleming, Ontario Ministry of Community and Social Services 1985), the known number of 332 nursing homes in 1983–84 involving 29,215 beds (Social Planning Council of Metro Toronto 1984, 31), and the data in Table 2.3 indicating a total of 628 special care facilities in Ontario in 1983 involving 61,237 beds. By subtracting the first two sets of these figures (182 and 28,000, and 332 and 29,215) from the totals for special care facilities (628

and 61,237) one arrives at an estimate of 114 residential care homes in
Ontario with about 4,000 beds. Alternatively, subtracting the nursing
home figures (332 and 29,215) from the numbers in Table 2.3 for proprietary auspices in Ontario (434 and 32,602) gives an estimate of 102
residential care homes with about 3,000 beds. However, the latter
estimates are only about half of the numbers for known members of the
Long-Term Residential Care Association of Ontario alone. These con-
tradictory figures illustrate the difficulties in determining the amount of
institutional care provided.

CHAPTER 3

A DEMOGRAPHIC PROFILE OF THE INSTITUTIONALIZED ELDERLY

3.1 PREVALENCE OF INSTITUTIONALIZATION AMONG THE ELDERLY IN CANADA

Table 3.1 gives data from the 1981 Census of Canada regarding the proportion of the total population that was over ages sixty-five and eighty-five (Statistics Canada 1982), and the proportion of people in those age groups who resided in long-term care institutions, utilizing census data regarding place of residence (Statistics Canada 1984b). Those over age sixty-five constituted 9.7% of the total population, 8.4% for males and 11.0% for females. The age group over eighty-five made up 0.8% of the total population, with the proportion of females, 1.1%, being more than double the proportion of males, 0.5%.

Table 3.1 shows that, while a negligible proportion of the population under age sixty-five (0.1%) resided in "Homes," the proportion increases sharply to 6.7% for those over sixty-five, with a rate in this age group of 4.7% for males and 8.2% for females. For those over age eighty-five, the proportion was substantially higher again at 32.5%, with a rate of 24.8% for males and 36.3% for females.

The figures for "Residing in Hospitals" in Table 3.1, as defined by census data, are considerably less than the numbers reported as "In Hospital at Beginning of Period" or "In Hospital at End of Period" for 1981–82 (Statistics Canada 1984c). The difference between these two sets of figures represents primarily those receiving acute care in hospitals. Hence, it seems reasonable to count all those in Table 3.1 who are "Residing in Hospitals," as residing in long-term care institutions. On that basis the sum of those Residing in Homes and those Residing in Hospitals in Table 3.1 will be used here as an estimate of the elderly population residing in long-term care institutions. This leads to an estimated 177,000 Canadians aged sixty-five and over residing in long-term care institutions in 1981, (7.5%), and 69,000 aged eighty-five and over (35.6%).

This rate of 7.5% is lower than the 8.8% given in Section 2.8 for the availability of beds for that age group in special care facilities and in extended care (including chronic care) hospitals. There are a number of reasons for the non-comparability of these two rates, among which are: (1) the former (7.5%) is for 1981, while the latter used a 1983 numerator and a 1981 denominator; (2) the former involves elderly persons considered in the census to be residents of long-term care institutions, while the latter involves beds in certain limited categories of long-term care institutions,

TABLE 3.1

TOTAL POPULATION AND POPULATION RESIDING IN HOMES[1] AND IN HOSPITALS,[2] FOR THE NON-ELDERLY AND THE ELDERLY, BY SEX, CANADA, 1981

Category	Age Group	Both Sexes	Males	Females
Total Population[3]				
Number (thousands)	Total	24,343	12,068	12,275
Number (thousands)	Under 65	21,982	11,057	10,925
Number (thousands)	65+	2,361	1,011	1,350
% of total population		9.7%	8.4%	11.0%
Number (thousands)	85+	194	64	130
% of total population		0.8%	0.5%	1.1%
Residing in Homes[1, 4]				
Number (thousands)	Total	185	62	123
% of total population		0.8%	0.5%	1.0%
Number (thousands)	Under 65	27	14	13
% of population under 65		0.1%	0.1%	0.1%
Number (thousands)	65+	158	48	110
% of population 65+		6.7%	4.7%	8.2%
Number (thousands)	85+	63	16	47
% of population 85+		32.5%	24.8%	36.3%
Residing in Hospitals[2, 4]				
Number (thousands)	Total	55	29	26
% of total population		0.2%	0.2%	0.2%
Number (thousands)	Under 65	36	21	15
% of population under 65		0.2%	0.2%	0.1%
Number (thousands)	65+	19	8	11
% of population 65+		0.8%	0.8%	0.8%
Number (thousands)	85+	6	2	4
% of population 85+		3.1%	3.1%	3.1%

1. Homes are defined as "nursing homes and institutions for the elderly and the chronically ill."
2. Hospitals are defined as "general hospitals, psychiatric institutions, treatment centres, and institutions for the handicapped."
3. Statistics Canada 1982.
4. Statistics Canada 1984b.

Reproduced with permission of the Minister of Supply and Services Canada.

some of which may not be occupied at any given time and many of which are occupied by younger residents. However, the former includes long-term care residents of all types of institutions, while the latter excludes long-term care beds in general and psychiatric hospitals.

Unfortunately, data from the 1961 and 1971 Canadian censuses comparable to that in Table 3.1 were not published. However, some data are available which estimate the nature of the trend in the prevalence of long-term care institutionalization among the elderly in Canada since 1961. Schwenger and Gross (1980) report that the percentage of persons age sixty-five and over who were in institutional care on any one day in Canada, including everyone in hospital care, increased from 7.7% in 1962–63 to 8.4% in 1976.[1]

The published table that gave the figures in Table 3.1 for "Residing in Homes" and "Residing in Hospitals" stated in a footnote that these data from the 1981 census were previously unpublished, and no breakdown by province was given. However, other data (Schwenger and Gross 1980) suggest how the provinces differ regarding the prevalence of institutionalization in the population over age sixty-five. Table 3.2 presents their data for 1976, as collected annually from institutions by Statistics Canada and complete for each province except Quebec, on the proportion of persons over age sixty-five who were "in various types of institutions at any given time." The overall prevalence rate of 8.4% given in Table 3.2 for the nine provinces differs from the estimate of 7.5% derived from census figures. Factors contributing to this difference include the fact that the former estimate is for persons "in institutions at any given time" (including acute care), while the latter is for persons "residing" in institutions (which is closer to the concept of institutionalization). Although the latter rate includes special care facilities in Quebec, the two estimates are five years apart. Despite the problem of obtaining accurate data, the difference between the provinces in Table 3.2, although not representing recent data, probably parallel the differences in the true prevalence rates of institutionalization, had the latter been available. The four adjacent central and western provinces, Ontario, Manitoba, Saskatchewan, and Alberta, had the highest rates, with Alberta having the highest (9.4%); Newfoundland had the lowest rate, 5.6%; and the four eastern provinces had generally lower rates.

The proportion of the elderly population which was aged eighty-five and over did not vary greatly between the provinces, and adjusting for this factor made little difference to the figures in Table 3.2. It can be concluded that the east-west differences are not because of differences between the provinces in the proportion of very old – those over age eighty-five. What factors may be responsible is not clear. Information on the year of initiation and scope of home care programs in the different provinces (Extended Health Care Services Program 1981) suggests that the lower proportions of elderly persons in institutions "at any given time" in 1976 in eastern prov-

TABLE 3.2

PROPORTION OF THE POPULATION OVER AGE SIXTY-FIVE IN
INSTITUTIONS AT ANY GIVEN TIME, FOR HOSPITALS AND FOR SPECIAL
CARE FACILITIES FOR THE CANADIAN PROVINCES, 1976

Province	Per Cent of Elderly Population (65+) In:		
	Hospitals[1]	Special Care Facilities	All Institutions[2]
Newfoundland	1.5	4.1	5.6
Prince Edward Island	1.5	6.4	7.9
Nova Scotia	1.9	5.2	7.1
New Brunswick	2.2	5.1	7.4
Quebec	3.1	–	–[3]
Ontario	2.4	6.5	8.9
Manitoba	2.6	6.5	9.1
Saskatchewan	2.4	6.3	8.7
Alberta	4.1	5.3	9.4
British Columbia	2.7	4.2	6.9
Total	2.7	5.8	8.4

1. Includes all General and Allied Special Hospitals (including Extended Care and Chronic Care Hospitals) and Mental Hospitals (Mental Health Facilities).

2. Hospitals plus Special Care Facilities. Totals may not be identical because of rounding.

3. See text, p. 39.

SOURCE: Adapted from Schwenger and Gross (1980, p. 250). Reproduced with permission of the publisher.

inces compared with central and western provinces was not because of a greater availability of home care services in the eastern provinces. Indeed, Schwenger (1985, 6–7) commented that:

> Most of the western provinces have progressed a great deal further than anywhere else in Canada in rationalizing their systems of long term care. This has involved the adoption of a social model with increasing recognition that social admissions are as important, frequently more important, than medical admissions. Control of the medical profession over the system has decreased and an attempt has been made to deprofessionalize home care. Continuing care has brought together provincial authorities responsible for long term care both at home and in institutions. Case management, assessment units and a single point of entry are all emphasized.

3.2 FACTORS ASSOCIATED WITH ADMISSION TO LONG-TERM CARE INSTITUTIONS

As indicated in the definitions of extended care and chronic care given in Section 2.3, persons receiving such care should have one or more chronic diseases and/or functional disabilities. The Ontario definition of residential care given in Section 2.3 requires that the recipient has decreased physical and/or mental faculties and needs supervision and/or assistance with activities of daily living. While anyone over age sixty can be admitted to a home for the aged in Ontario without associated chronic disease, disability, or functional deficits, very few such admissions actually occur any more.

It was found in the Rochester, N.Y. area in the late 1960s (Berg et al. 1970a) that forgetfulness and confusion were the main factors in the inability of old persons to continue living independently. An Ontario study (Kraus et al. 1976a) reported that 40% of elderly applicants to long-term care institutions (mostly homes for the aged) had Dementia Scale scores of 5 or more (on a scale of 0 to 10), compared with 4% of elderly persons living independently in the community. Two longitudinal studies, in Massachusetts (Branch and Jette 1982) and in Manitoba (Shapiro and Tate 1985) both noted that mental impairment among the elderly was a significant predictor of eventual long-term care facility use.

Kraus also showed that a number of other specific health-related factors were more common among elderly applicants to long-term care institutions than among elderly persons living independently in the community, namely: (1) self-rating of current health as poor (28%:3%); (2) two or more chronic disorders or important health problems reported (81%:52%); (3) much trouble controlling bladder or bowels ("accidents") (19%:2%); (4) need for direct help with certain activities of daily living, or the inability to perform them even with help, e.g., dressing or undressing (34%:1%); and (5) hospitalization in the previous year (72%:13%). Branch and Jette found that the use of ambulation aids and the need for assistance in activities of daily living were significantly associated with subsequent long-term care institutionalization. Shapiro and Tate found that being admitted to hospital in the year of the initial interview and having one or more problems with basic activities of daily living were significant predictors of admission to a long-term care facility (see also Section 5.1).

Advanced age and health status are not the only variables that are related to admission to a long-term care institution. A major predictive demographic factor is that of "living arrangements" or "household composition." Kraus et al. (1976a) found that living with a spouse was much less frequent among applicants to institutions than among the elderly living in the community who had not applied for admission to an institution (19%:56%), while living alone was somewhat more frequent among the applicants to institutions (35%:26%); (see also Branch and Jette 1982 and Shapiro and Tate 1985). The availability of female relatives to provide assistance is believed to be another factor (see Section 4.1). Kraus et al. noted that being in the lowest family income category was more common among applicants to institutions than among the elderly non-applicants (53%:16%). He also observed, however (Kraus 1984), that some seriously demented elderly persons continue to live at home despite severe physical, mental and behavioural problems and needs for care that one would ordinarily expect to have resulted in institutionalization. This tends to occur if the key care-giving relative feels strongly about keeping the dementia victim at home and out of an institution (see also Shanas 1979).

The relationship between admission to a long-term care institution and having lived alone or without a spouse probably plays an important role in the previously cited higher rate of long-term care institutionalization among elderly women compared with elderly men. Wilkins and Adams (1983, 26) comment that:

> ... elderly men are more likely than elderly women to have a surviving spouse capable of providing them with basic care. Should their health become impaired it is thus easier for men than women to continue living at home.

It may also be noted that widowers are more likely to remarry than widows.

Among the changes which have taken place, there is evidence that residents of chronic care hospitals tend to be older than in the past. To illustrate this point from Ontario, special tabulations were obtained from the Ontario Ministry of Health regarding the age distribution at admission and the length of stay of all patients who had been discharged (including deaths) from the chronic care hospitals in 1983–84 and in 1979–80, and who were aged sixty-five and over when admitted to the hospital (Ontario Ministry of Health 1985).[2]

These tabulations showed that there was a small increase in the average age at admission from 79.38 years for those discharged in 1979–80 to 79.80 years for those discharged in 1983–84, and that the proportion of those discharges who were eighty-five years and older at admission increased from 26.7% to 29.0% during this four-year period. (The 8.6% relative increase in the latter proportion is considerably greater than the 1.8% increase between the 1976 and 1981 censuses in the proportion of the Ontario population over age sixty-five which was eighty-five and older; Statistics Canada 1979 and 1982). The reasons for these changes may be that the elderly are able to remain longer in the community because they are healthier, because of more extensive community services, including supportive housing, or because of an increased annual income. Another reason may be that it is more difficult to gain admission; however it is conceivable that the data only represent fluctuations and do not represent a trend.

Another tabulation showed a decrease between the two years in the proportion of discharges whose length of stay in the chronic care hospital had been under one year (from 87.2% for 1979–80 discharges to 83.4% for 1983–84 discharges). There was also a small increase in the proportion of those who were dead at discharge (34.6%:36.1%). These latter two trends, suggesting longer stays and poorer health, for all chronic care hospitals in Ontario are in contrast to those observed in one hospital after introduction of new programs of care, as noted in Section 7.1 (Schuman et al. 1978; 1980).

3.3 THE PREVALENCE OF INSTITUTIONALIZATION IN CANADA AND OTHER COUNTRIES

It is difficult on the basis of the available material to reach any sound conclusion about how the prevalence rate of institutionalization among the elderly in Canada compares with that in other developed countries. On the one hand, Schwenger and Gross (1980) compare Canada with Great Britain and the United States, in both the early 1960s and in the 1970s, regarding the "Percentage of Persons 65+ in Institutional Care on Any One Day." Their data suggest that Canada had higher prevalence rates than the other two countries. Their rates for Canada, 7.7% and 8.4%, respectively (also cited in Section 3.1), are higher than the rates for Great Britain, 4.6% and 5.1%, respectively (the latter for England and Wales only), and for the United States, 4.7% and 6.3%, respectively. These figures were obtained from separate sources within each country, each of which had used varying definitions and methods. Schwenger and Gross acknowledge (p. 251) that "caution is again advised because of differences in geography, difficulties of definitions, methodology, and particularly, time intervals." Nevertheless, Schwenger and Gross consider Canada's rate as being high, and ask why this should be so (p. 252). In discussing the answer to this question, they cite Canada's "general tendency ... to institutionalize our 'deviant' citizens, be they criminals or invalids, young or old," as well as factors such as geography, climate, population mobility, and new work roles for women, who might otherwise have been providers of care to the elderly at home. They also refer to the "bias of our health insurance scheme" in Canada, which did not insure home-care services as early as it insured hospital and institutional care. This policy differed from that in Great Britain, where these services were insured simultaneously under the National Health Service.

On the other hand, British investigators (Grundy and Arie 1984) utilized national censuses in the 1970s as the primary source of data, and found a different picture. They report that the proportion of persons sixty-five years and over who were "in medical and social welfare institutions" in 1971 was 4.3% in Canada versus 4.8% in England and Wales. Still higher rates were found for four other countries: Israel, Japan, France, and New Zealand, in ascending order, with the latter reaching 6.6% in 1971. A similar pattern was present in the "Standardized Institutional Ratios" (SIR) calculated for the same countries, which eliminated the effect of differences between the countries in the sex-age composition of their populations. England and Wales afforded an SIR of 100.0, Canada an SIR of 86.31, while the SIR for the other four countries ranged from 114.1 for Japan to 134.8 for New Zealand. Thus, according to this study, among these six countries, Canada had the lowest prevalence of institutionalization among the elderly, independent of the effect of sex-age differences in the composition of the population. No significant association was found by Grundy and Arie between the SIRs in these countries and the demographic variables of males per 1,000 females aged seventy-five and older, or the percentage never married among persons aged seventy-five and older. The variations in SIRs were also unrelated to variations in gross national product per capita; to the proportion of the elderly who were economically active; to the proportion of the total economically active population employed in agriculture, fishing, or forestry; or, to the earnings replacement rate (pension as a percentage of earnings in the year before retirement).

Schwenger and Gross attempted to obtain data on "persons in institutional care on any one day," a method which has also been used in other studies (Preston 1986), whereas Grundy and Arie used national census data to obtain data on "persons in institutions." The latter presumably meant persons counted as residents of institutions in the censuses, which may be a major factor in explaining the lower rates reported by Grundy and Arie compared with those reported by Schwenger and Gross. However, the Grundy and Arie rate (4.8%) for England and Wales in 1971, is only a little less than the Schwenger and Gross rate of 5.1%, while the Grundy and Arie rate for Canada (4.3%) in 1971, is markedly lower than the Schwenger and Gross rate for either 1962–63 (7.7%) or 1976 (8.4%) or the rate of 7.5% derived in Section 3.1 from the 1981 census. The reasons for these discrepancies are not apparent. The Grundy and Arie rate for Canada appears suspiciously low, in comparison with what has been presented in this chapter and in Chapter 2. It is difficult, therefore, to conclude how the prevalence rate of institutionalization among the elderly in Canada compares with that in other developed countries.

As indicated in Section 3.1, the trend in the prevalence rate of institutionalization of the elderly in Canada has been upward, at least through 1981. This increase is greater than would be expected from the increase in the proportion of the very old. Census data for England and Wales show that the proportion of persons "in institutions on census day" changed little between 1951 and 1971 in the sixty-five to sixty-nine, seventy to seventy-four, and seventy-five to seventy-nine age groups in each sex, but increased substantially in the eighty and over group for each sex, particularly among females (Evans 1977, 130–31). This increase in the eighty and older group was due primarily to the increased proportion residing in "Residential Homes." Evans believes that this increase "may reflect an increase in social need since owing to a fall in birth rate between the Wars the average number of potentially dutiful middle-aged children available to give support to elderly parents fell by 19% during this period ...." Further, he predicted that this process will continue throughout the twentieth century. He suggests that increasing widowhood rates and the outward migration of younger families may contribute also to a decline in family support. The role of community support programs and services in preventing or delaying the institutionalization of the elderly is clearly important. This topic will be discussed in Chapter 4, together with the types of such programs and services.

3.4 SUMMARY AND CONCLUSIONS

Following the description in Chapter 2 of the various types of long-term care facilities which are available, the present chapter discusses the proportions of elderly in these institutions. One question of interest is how these proportions for Canada compare with those in other countries. The data also show that there are variations within Canada. This then leads to an examination of the factors associated with institutionalization, and a number of these can be identified. One of the factors which is important is the relationship between services offered in institutions and community support programs. This issue will be addressed in Chapter 4.

The following may be concluded:

1. Although there are strong indications that the Canadian rate of institutionalization is relatively high, published reports are not consistent, and a firm conclusion regarding this issue cannot be reached.
2. The trend in the prevalence of institutionalization among the elderly during the last two decades appears to have been upward in both Canada, and England and Wales, beyond what can be attributed to the aging of the population.
3. Associated with institutionalization of the elderly are health, demographic, socioeconomic and psychological factors, as well as advanced age itself.

NOTES

1. See Section 3.3 for further discussion of factors contributing to this trend.
2. It was not possible to obtain tabulations for all elderly admissions prior to 1979–80.

CHAPTER 4

THE COMMUNITY-INSTITUTION
INTERFACE

In the not too distant past there was a marked division between the community and institutions for the elderly. Elderly men and women continued to live in the community as long as they were able to be independent. If illness or disability interfered with their independence, and no friends or relatives were available to provide assistance, the only solution was institutional care, a move which often involved, and may still involve, a final and complete separation from their community. This situation has changed in some ways with the expansion of community support services. Although community long-term care will not be discussed in detail in this monograph, it is impossible to ignore non-institutional services provided for the elderly, particularly those who are frail, since the presence or lack of those services often affects the need for institutionalization. Moreover, programs and services such as day hospitals, day care, vacation care and placement co-ordination services, involve a sharing of responsibilities for the frail elderly between institutions and the community. Thus, this chapter does not aim to review all the community services or housing options that may be used by older adults, but considers some of those which may affect the decision to seek institutional care. (For a recent discussion of housing options for the elderly in Canada, see Gutman and Blackie 1986.)

There is a growing recognition that flexibility should exist throughout the range of community and institutional services and that this should constitute a two-way street. Although for many, increasing disabilities will imply an increasing need for assistance, the often-mentioned "continuum of care" should ease not only progression from one level of care to the next, but also a change to a different type of service, or a reduction in the level of care needed. The growing emphasis on rehabilitation and the monitoring of patients makes the latter course, at least in theory, more of an option than was previously the case.

These new approaches are due partly to the need to reduce expensive institutional care, based on the belief that community care is less expensive (but see Section 4.4), and due partly to humanitarian reasons concerning the quality of life and patients' rights (see also Section 6.3). Whatever the reason, the questioning and reassessment of accepted modes of treatment and care are valuable.

4.1 COMMUNITY CARE IN RELATION TO INSTITUTIONAL CARE

A range of services for senior citizens exists in many communities throughout Canada. Although all may be important, the ones which are most closely related to institutional care are those services which provide support to elderly people in their daily personal and domestic activities. Most of the elderly remain active and independent, but functional ability does tend to decline with age. Various surveys (Fryer and Piercey 1981; Jackson and Forbes 1986; Stolee et al. 1982) suggest that up to 12% of the elderly living in the community need assistance with activities such as dressing, washing, and preparing a meal, and as many as 25% need help with housework and shopping. These needs are usually met by family members, most frequently by the spouse or a female relative (Aronson 1985; Jackson and Forbes 1986). However, it has been shown that many old people have extensive networks of friends, neighbours and more distant relatives who provide assistance (Cantor 1983; Chappell 1985; Chappell and Havens 1985). Often assistance is reciprocated in some form by the elderly individual (Chappell and Havens 1985; Rosenthal 1986; Shanas 1979).

It is important to emphasize that those requiring assistance tend to be amongst the oldest members of the population, seventy-five years and older. A corollary of this is the fact that those family members most likely to be providing assistance, the spouse, children or siblings, may themselves be elderly. Home care and homemakers' services (see below) are available in most provinces, but decisions regarding provision of community services are often affected by the availability of family assistance (Béland 1986; Connidis 1985; Havens 1986, 79). Another factor in the provision of community services are the financial resources of a municipality. The less affluent ones are unable to finance their share of the cost, which deprives them of access to provincial and federal dollars (personal communication, Mrs. S. Goldblatt 1987).

Eligibility for home care and homemaker programs, as well as the components of them, vary from province to province (Lang and Shelton 1982, 36–48). Initially home-care programs were intended for acute care, usually for patients who had been discharged from hospital, but later they were extended for those needing chronic care. Such programs may provide a variety of health treatment and support services to persons in their own homes, including nursing care, physiotherapy, occupational, respiratory and speech therapy, medical supplies and drugs. Homemaking, handyman services, meals-on-wheels, and the support of a social worker may also be provided. Chiropody services, which are legally required in the United

Kingdom, are not common, and foot care is usually provided by the nurse. The first universal, free-to-consumers, home-care program in Canada was initiated in Manitoba in 1974 and expanded throughout the province in 1975 (Havens 1986, 78). In some provinces such as Alberta, Newfoundland and, until recently, Ontario, a person, to qualify for acute or chronic home care, must require a "medical" service, as determined by the assessment of a physician or other health professional. This, and other restrictions such as the minimum number of hours of service per visit imposed by some programs, may limit their usefulness for the elderly who, despite their chronic disabilities, may not require a professional health-care service, nor the minimum number of hours of homemaking provided by the program. However, an increasing number of provinces are now offering either chronic home-care programs which do not have such restrictions, or separate homemaking programs. The general policy, for example, of the British Columbia home-care (Long-Term Care) program and Manitoba's home-care (Continuing Care) program is to provide community support services within the client's home unless the cost of those services would exceed the cost of similar care in an institutional setting (Lang and Shelton 1982, 38, 41).

Homemaking services can perform a variety of functions, including housekeeping, some shopping, light meals, assistance with personal care, and heavy house cleaning, in addition to the social contact and emotional support involved in regular visits. Elderly people form the large majority of a home-help agency's case load. The provision of home-help aides, or homemakers, across Canada is expanding with services in all provinces and the Northwest Territories, but the number still remains short of that recommended elsewhere. In the United Kingdom, for example, official guidelines call for 1.5 full-time equivalent (F.T.E) home-help aides per thousand population (Latto 1982, 65) compared to an estimate in the early 1980s of 0.5 per thousand in Canada.[1] Other European countries such as Norway, Sweden and the Netherlands had extensive home-help services even in 1976 (see Table 4.1), and may also provide evening, night and weekend services. However, even in these countries there is concern that social service resources are not keeping pace with the growth in the older, frail population (Nusberg 1984, 117–19). The disparity between countries in the provision of home-help services is indicated in Table 4.1, but these figures are of only limited value since not only has there been considerable expansion of these services in recent years in Canada and elsewhere, but also the number of hours worked, the level of training, and the proportion of the population aged sixty-five and older are not provided.

Lack of adequate training of homemakers was one of the chief problems identified in one survey (Canadian Council on Homemaker Services 1982). This issue is relevant to the type of work and level of responsibility required. All the agencies responding felt that training was necessary, yet thirty-two agencies provided no orientation and another twenty-three did

TABLE 4.1

HOME HELPERS PER 100,000 IN SELECTED COUNTRIES, DECEMBER 1976

Country	Total Population (thousands)	Number of Home Helpers	Number Per 100,000
Austria	7,525	340	4.5
Belgium	9,957	8,661	87.0
Canada	22,000	3,290	15.0
Germany (Federal Republic)	60,000	12,685	22.0
Finland	4,500	6,073	135.0
France	50,000	7,144	14.3
Great Britain	49,000	129,724	265.0
Israel	3,300	350	10.6
Italy	54,000	50	0.1
Japan	111,934	8,706	7.7
Netherlands	13,800	82,700	599.0
Norway	3,988	33,478	840.0
Sweden	8,220	74,900	923.0
Switzerland	6,000	2,505	41.7
United States	209,000	60,000	28.7

SOURCE: Charlotte Nusberg, with Mary Jo Gibson and Sheila Peace, *Innovative Aging Programs Abroad: Implications for the United States* (Greenwood Press, Inc., Westport, CT. 1984), p. 118. Copyright © 1984 by the International Federation on Ageing. Used by permission of the publisher.

not reply to the question. Among the other responding agencies, the orientation ranged from a mean of 7.3 hours for the proprietary agencies to a mean of 20 hours for non-profit, multi-service agencies. In-service group training sessions were provided by almost all the agencies (95%), but nearly half of them did so only "occasionally." Another training option, a home-making course offered by a community college or other resource, was available in the locality for only 58% of the agencies.

In comparison to this limited and variable level of training provided in Canada, European countries are increasingly providing formal training for all home-help aides. In Denmark, for example, all home-help aides must have seven weeks of training in their first six months of employment and additional courses later. In addition, the range of duties and responsibilities given to home-help aides is expanding. The "extra-hospital aide" in Geneva, Switzerland, has duties between those of a traditional home-help aide and those of a "practical nurse," while in the United Kingdom some jurisdictions are using the aide as a key liaison with the health services. Case conferences, team work, use of aides for simple home nursing, responsibility for helping clients to help themselves, are all changing the image of the home-help aide.

Other models, such as having heavy cleaning done by men equipped with heavy-duty cleaning tools, and the establishment of home-care centres staffed with home-help aides and nurses who can be called in an emergency, are expanding the ways in which the elderly can be helped to remain at home (Nusberg 1984, 118–19).

Although community long-term care programs have not been in operation in Canada as long as they have been in many European countries, there is evidence that they have been successful in preventing or delaying institutionalization of elderly clients (Kraus and Armstrong 1977; Kraus et al. 1982; Nocks et al. 1986), and in reducing long-term care costs (Health and Welfare Canada 1982). However, the effect of these programs is that those who are eventually admitted to a residential facility are often older, more frail and disabled than hitherto (see Section 3.2). Partly because most people wish to remain in the familiarity and independence of their own homes and communities for as long as possible (Connidis 1983; Shanas 1979; Wister 1985), an important question is the extent and nature of care likely to be needed by elderly people in the future. This question also has implications for the architecture, staffing, equipping and programming of old age and nursing homes.

4.2 PLACEMENT CO-ORDINATION SERVICES: COUNSELLING AND ASSESSMENT SERVICES

One of the recurring problems for elderly people, their families, health professionals and institutions regarding institutional admission has been the identification of an available and appropriate placement. Individuals have been inappropriately placed (Cape et al. 1977; Kraus et al. 1976b), either in an environment where they were not able to receive adequate care, or alternatively where they received more care than was necessary (see Section 2.8). The difficulty of obtaining a suitable bed arises because of a variety of problems. Placement is determined by what is available at an affordable price. Unfortunately, institutional placement often involves a hurried decision, occurring at a time of crisis, rather than being considered carefully and planned in advance. Such admission frequently results in an inappropriate placement in an institution which may also be inconveniently located for visits from the patient's family and friends. This may compound the trauma often experienced by the elderly person who has his or her life and routine disrupted so abruptly (Grant 1985a; Schulz and Brenner 1977).

Attempts are being made to overcome these problems, within the limits of program availability. Many organizations and senior citizens centres have been providing information, counselling and referral resources for the elderly and their families. Public health nurses also have an important role in providing advice and monitoring the health and social circumstances of their elderly clients. However, none of these services avoid the need for the individual or family to apply to each facility individually in search of a place, which can be a confusing and frustrating procedure. To simplify the process of locating an appropriate bed, placement co-ordination and similar services have been established. The first formal comprehensive placement service in Canada was established in Hamilton-Wentworth in 1971 (Bayne and Caygill 1977), and since then other areas have developed similar services. The intent of these services is to match the applicant with the most appropriate and most desired placement. The operation of the placement co-ordination service may vary from area to area, but basically each receives applications for long-term care placements from community physicians or other health professionals, from hospital discharge planners or from long-term care facilities themselves. At the same time the service maintains an up-to-date list of beds available, and of their characteristics, within its area of operation. Assessment of the applicant and the level of care needed may be carried out by the client's physician, or by a team of health professionals. Assessment of the applicant by a health-care team within his or her home, with its familiar surroundings, provides not only a more detailed and accurate assessment but also may prevent institutionalization since the team members, with their knowledge of the community, may be able to recommend support services not considered by the client or family.[2] In Ontario, placement co-ordination services are sponsored locally by planning or service agencies and are funded by the Ministry of Health (Lang and Shelton 1982, 72). There are currently fifteen in operation in the province (personal communication, R. Youtz, Office Director, Community Health Programs Branch, Ontario Ministry of Health 1986).

A rather different system (see also Section 2.9) is in operation in Manitoba, which, as mentioned in the previous section, provided the first universal province-wide home-care program in Canada. The Office of Continuing Care was established in 1974, and there are regional offices in each of the province's eight health regions. The program aims to identify and support those people who, without services, would be at risk of being admitted to an institution but who, with home-delivered services, could have their care needs managed appropriately. People may be referred for home care or extended care by a health professional or a family member. Applications, completed by physicians, other health professionals and family members, are reviewed by a panel which assesses whether the applicant can be maintained at a home with appropriate support services. If this is not possible, the panel will determine the level of care needed (Health and Welfare Canada 1982).

Another provincial program which incorporates long-term institutional and home-care services is that established in 1978 by the Ministry of Health in British Columbia (Robertson 1982, 209). Applicants are assessed, using a comprehensive form, by a case manager, who may be a registered nurse, occupational therapist or medical social worker. A local health-unit team decides the extent, type and place of service needed, maintaining the client at home if possible. A single waiting list is maintained by the long-term care program for "opted-in" facilities in the region, and the system attempts to offer maximum choice to the client and the facility.

A related service available in a number of areas is the geriatric assessment unit or centre (Robertson 1982, 205–6). These may be located in acute care hospitals, geriatric hospitals or extended care facilities. For example, there are three in British Columbia which are funded by the Long Term Care Program of the Ministry of Health and more are planned. Manitoba has three such programs operating in hospitals, while another unit exists in Saskatoon (Lang and Shelton 1982, 67, 73). Hospitals in other provinces are also establishing geriatric assessment units. These centres admit elderly people for periods of two to four weeks during which time a thorough medical and functional assessment is made (see also Section 4.3). In some cases the unit may be associated with a facility having long-term care beds, but elsewhere there may be no special access to such beds.

Assessments may also be carried out on an out-patient basis at day hospitals and clinics. These units provide not only assessment preparatory to long-term care in the community or institutions, but also a monitoring function for elderly people living in the community. It is claimed that many remediable problems can be identified in this way (Rubenstein et al. 1986). New problems may be recognized and treated, and chronic conditions stabilized so that deterioration and possibly institutionalization can be avoided. Nevertheless, all of these programs, however valuable, will need the general acceptance of the elderly client, his or her family and the family physician, all of whom may perceive the programs as involving loss of personal choice.

4.3 OUTREACH PROGRAMS

Long-term care facilities can also be involved in various outreach programs which link the activities and services of the institution with the elderly living in the community. Some residential-care facilities now run or are associated with day-care centres and occasionally day hospitals. The former provide supervison, social contacts, recreational activities and some personal care for frail, moderately handicapped or confused elderly people and, at the same time, relieve the older person's family from total responsibility. Lang and Shelton (1982, 36–48, 75) reported day-care programs operating within nursing homes or other residential facilities in Alberta, Manitoba, New Brunswick, Ontario, Prince Edward Island, Saskatchewan and the Yukon. Other day-care programs in these provinces and elsewhere operate from non-residential locations. Fees for participants range from no charge to about five dollars per day, with subsidies or grants being provided by provincial ministries.

Day hospitals (Tucker 1982) provide therapeutic and rehabilitation programs as well as the assessment and monitoring facilities mentioned previously (Section 4.2). In some areas, the geriatric day hospital may have a custodial or social role as well as a remedial one. Day hospitals are more likely to be associated with an acute care hospital, but in some cases operate independently or within long-term care institutions. The presence of day hospitals in nursing homes in the Netherlands is reported to have accelerated patient turnover (Nusberg 1984, 69), and temporary closure of a geriatric day hospital is said to have increased acute hospital admissions and deaths among the elderly clients (Berrey 1986). Referral by a physician is usually necessary for acceptance in a day hospital program, but is not normally required for a day-care centre.

Another service provided by a growing number of long-term care institutions is that of respite or vacation-relief beds. The institution maintains a limited number of beds for short-term admission, which temporarily relieves the family or other caregiver of responsibility and makes a rest or vacation possible. For heavily burdened family members caring for a frail and confused elderly person, this period of relief and the knowledge of support available in a crisis, may make all the difference in preventing institutionalization (but see Scharlach and Frenzel 1986; Zorzitto et al. 1986). The program can also help the elderly client to become familiar with the institution, staff and other residents, which may be of benefit if emergency or permanent admission becomes necessary. The length of stay is usually two or three weeks, with the date of discharge agreed on between the physician, family and institution before admission.

In some centres such short-term stays are used to evaluate the elderly person's medical and functional status, and to monitor medications. An extension of this idea is a program in which a few beds in a geriatric unit are reserved for elderly patients who are admitted on a regular basis for a few days (Robertson et al. 1977). This use of one bed may help to maintain several individuals in the community. Some institutions in Canada believe that these programs are too costly for them since it involves additional organization, as well as keeping one or more beds empty that could be needed by patients awaiting admission. However, it seems likely that these difficulties could be overcome if the service was more widely publicized and used more effectively.[3]

In the United Kingdom and other European countries, respite-care beds often cannot meet the demand and other options have been established, such as short-term homes and respite foster care (Gibson 1984, 173). In Canada, respite or vacation care is available in residential-care facilities in most if not all of the provinces, but in general the provision seems to be limited to the larger urban areas. Lang and Shelton (1982, 67) reported that, in Manitoba, five facilities had beds set aside for respite care, Newfoundland had three and Saskatchewan four facilities. In Prince Edward Island three out of 500 beds in public homes were set aside for respite care, while New Brunswick had approximately fourteen to eighteen such beds. Interestingly, the government of New Brunswick has suggested that one bed in every fifty new places in nursing homes should be set aside for relief care.

There are also "half-way houses" that aim to prepare residents for a return to the community. In these, residents live in small group homes associated with a residential-care facility. Residents are relatively independent but may need occasional assistance with personal care or medications, and they have the use of the facilities and services of the institution. An example of this type of program is the "Pavillon" in Quebec (Lang and Shelton 1982, 72). Another program, found in the United Kingdom, is the assessment apartment. A resident who is being considered for discharge, lives independently for a period of six to eight weeks in a small unit or apartment associated with the institution. A team of health professionals provides assistance and support while assessing the client's capabilities with independent living. Strong motivation on the part of the client, careful selection, and the availability of suitable accommodation at the end of the assessment have been found to be essential for the success of the scheme.

In the Regional Municipality of Niagara, Ontario, a foster home program, developed under the auspices of the local homes for the aged, enables elderly people to be boarded in private homes (Rapelje 1981, 212). The program is referred to as Private Home Care and places one to five elderly people in private homes under the supervision of the hostess/proprietor. A private bedroom, meals and laundry are provided but the residents are encouraged to help with light housework and to look after their own rooms. The eligibility criteria for the program are the same as those for admission to the homes for the aged. About a quarter of the residents also qualify for extended care. With relatively stable physical and mental health and the support provided in the foster homes, these senior citizens have been able to remain in the community. The hostess is reassured by the knowledge that medical services, including admission if necessary, can be provided through the sponsoring home for the aged. Similarly, in Quebec, Community Social Service Centres recruit, train and supervise foster families (Famille d'Accueil) who may take a maximum of nine guests needing assistance with personal care (Lang and Shelton 1982, 72).

Many other programs provide support to the elderly and their families and link long-term care institutions with the community. For example, residents of long-term care facilities operate programs such as "Telecheck" in which they maintain regular telephone contact with lonely and isolated seniors living in the community. In another program, elderly but relatively healthy and active residents of a home for the aged visit retarded and disabled children in a local Home. They provide a valuable contact for these disabled youngsters and some assistance for the staff. Long-term care institutions also provide meals from their kitchens for the local meals-on-wheels program.

The need for discussion and support groups for the families of frail elderly people is being recognized increasingly. Staff of long-term care facilities are among those who are organizing and running such groups, both for families of the facility's residents and for relatives of those still living in the community. The Maimonides Hospital and Home for the Aged in Montreal developed a program in 1978 to help family members discuss and come to terms with the decision to institutionalize a relative. This has become an important service offered to families of those awaiting admission. Groups organized for family members of residents not only help the relatives with their feelings of distress, confusion and guilt, but also help them to understand behavioural changes which may occur, and provide suggestions of ways to maintain and improve communication with a confused and sometimes resentful elderly person. The staff of facilities that encourage interaction between staff, relatives and residents believe that the benefits in mutual understanding and support, resident involvement and general morale outweigh the extra staff time (Gibson 1984, 175–77; Kramer and Kramer 1976, 135). This may be particularly important in the early months following admission of an elderly person.

4.4 EFFECTIVENESS OF COMMUNITY SUPPORT PROGRAMS

The community programs outlined in Sections 4.1–4.3 provide an essential service. Indeed their value has seemed so apparent that few comparative studies or evaluations of their effectiveness have been carried out. Also there is difficulty in designing research capable of providing rigorous evaluation. Gross and Schwenger (1981, 82) provide several references to articles which discuss the advantages of various community care programs, including home care, day hospitals and foster homes. Provision of care by these services is believed to be more humane and effective as well as being what older people prefer but, as Gross and Schwenger point out, it has not been shown that community services are always less expensive than an equivalent level of institutional care. There are also problems in defining what is meant by "effective" in the context of community health and social programs (see also Section 6.9). Cost effectiveness is an important aspect but the contribution which a program makes to a range of services, the extent to which those services promote an "age-integrated" society, provide varied services to a heterogeneous group, and enhance the quality of life for the elderly are also important. Chappell et al. (1986, 128–32), who have reviewed work done on the evalution of community programs and highlight some of the difficulties involved in conducting such research, conclude that existing evaluations provide support for the effectiveness of community social programs but are not conclusive.

As mentioned in Section 4.1, chronic home care can delay or prevent institutionalization. The question is whether home care is always appropriate or cost effective. Opit (1977) studied a hundred and thirty-nine patients in Birmingham, England, who were receiving domiciliary nursing and other community services. He estimated that 20% of his sample were more expensive to manage at home than in a geriatric hospital. Furthermore, Opit believes that in some cases the support provided was either inadequate or inappropriate. As many as 30% of the sample, many of them severely disabled, were believed to be receiving unsatisfactory levels of care.

Opit and others (see Doherty and Hicks 1975; Gerson and Hughes 1976) have noted the difficulty of estimating the full costs of community services. Service costs may be based only on contact time with the client, and indirect costs associated with maintaining a home, and assistance provided by family or friends may be ignored.[4] Nusberg (1984, 184) refers to an estimate, from the Health Care Financing Administration in the United States, that "between 60 percent and 80 percent of the care received by the impaired elderly is provided by family members who are not compensated, and the value of services rises with the level of impairment." Opit emphasizes that the decision to treat a patient at home or in an institution cannot be made only on economic grounds, but points out that this factor cannot be dismissed. A study of home care in Manitoba (Health and Welfare Canada 1982) indicated that the cost saving of a comprehensive universal home-care program (see Section 4.1), over the alternative level of institutional care which would be needed if home care were not available, can be substantial (see also Hu et al. 1986). On average, the savings in the Manitoba program increased with the higher levels of institutional care that would have been needed. However, the program is designed to provide the minimum services required to meet need and to foster independence (Havens 1986, 79). Where additional assistance is provided by family or friends, the true financial and personal costs may be higher than realized.

Examination of only the cost of home-care services may ignore other factors. Lack of adequate funding may mean that the services supplied are not the best, that there are limited staff and equipment, and therefore some clients receive inadequate or no services (Opit 1977). Tinker (see Nusberg 1984, 129) comments that it is those already receiving one service who are likely to apply for others, while those with the greatest needs may not obtain all the help they require. Studies by Shanas (1971; 1974) suggest that in a number of countries the proportion of bedridden aged persons living at home is as great or greater than those in institutions. Questions have been raised about the ability of community services to grow to meet this potential need. In many countries social services depend on volunteers, and it may not be possible to continue some services economically as more women enter full-time work.[5]

It has been asked whether the availability of community social services removes responsibility from families and thus discourages them from helping their elderly relatives. However Gibson (1984, 181–84) cites several studies which conclude that the majority of families do not reduce their level of support, but are assisted by community services in caring for relatives (see also Brody 1981; Brody and Schoonover 1986; Chappell 1985; Chappell et al. 1986, 147–50). The suggestion that families should be encouraged through financial incentives to provide more care for their elderly relatives may be helpful in some cases, but in general ignores the evidence that families are already providing a great deal of assistance, even in the presence of many problems (Andrews et al. 1985) and financial strains are not the main issue (Cantor 1983; see also Section 7.1).

Other issues, such as the availability of a variety of housing options, affect the ability of services to maintain the elderly living independently in the community. Problems of communication and co-ordination also affect the extent to which community services can meet the needs of elderly people. Co-ordination between agencies is particularly important when the elderly have limited mobility and needs in many interrelated areas. The abundance of programs causes confusion among providers and recipients of care. Provision of a range of services within one centre, as has been done in Finland (Finland 1982, 31) and at the Baycrest Centre for Geriatric Care in Toronto, is one solution, but may not be generally feasible. The Finns interestingly, have found it more economical to transport clients to a centre than to provide services in their homes. Also some programs, such as placement co-ordination services and counselling services, may be limited in their effectiveness by a poor range of other services, and by a reluctance of other agencies to co-ordinate their activities. Centralized co-ordination of both institutional and community services as is done in Manitoba and British Columbia seems to overcome many of these difficulties.

4.5 SUMMARY AND CONCLUSIONS

There is little doubt that community-based services for the elderly will expand in response to a growing perceived need for such services, and that they constitute an important alternative to institutionalization of the elderly. Nusberg (1984) refers to many community support programs available in Europe, which are less developed, or not yet developed, in North America. In this chapter, a number of community-care services are described, including home care and homemaking services, placement co-ordination services, geriatric assessment units, and outreach programs such as day hospitals, respite or vacation-relief beds, foster home programs, and half-way or assessment apartments. Various social programs linking residents of long-term care institutions with the community are also mentioned.

Providing an adequate level and quality of service is costly. It is probable that there will always be waiting lists (see Section 6.7.1), that priorities must be set, and guidelines established to indicate where domiciliary services are not only more expensive than institutional care, but also not in the best interest of the client and his or her family. A willingness to experiment will be needed and a readiness to replace rigid established systems by new imaginative options without reducing the quality of care (see Section 7.1). There will also be a need to justify the introduction and continuation of programs. In future, studies using more rigorous methodology will be required so that decisions can be made on the basis of reliable information.

Community support services are not a universal substitute for institutional care of the frail elderly, but comprehensive, well-co-ordinated community programs can achieve much in maintaining elderly individuals in their own or relatives' homes. However, for a certain proportion of the elderly, this is not practically or financially feasible. The challenge is to provide varied and flexible community programs associated with a range of institutional settings which, together, can ensure the availability of appropriate support.

The following may be concluded:

1. Community-based services of the elderly have an important role to play and can delay or prevent institutionalization.
2. The concept of a continuum of care linking the community and institutions should be encouraged.
3. There are substantial differences in community-based services available in different parts of Canada. These services include a large variety of programs, including home care and homemaking services, placement co-ordination services, geriatric assessment units or centres, day hospitals, respite or vacation-relief beds, foster home programs, half-way or assessment apartments, and outreach programs.

   Such programs are operated in different ways in different regions and countries. It is likely that there is no single most effective way to implement these programs, since this will depend on other services available, as well as on social, cultural, geographic and other factors.
4. Considerations of only the cost of home-care services may ignore other factors, but the cost-effectiveness of the various programs cannot be neglected.

NOTES

1. Based on a survey in the early 1980s of homemakers' services (Canadian Council on Homemaker Services 1982) it was estimated that there were

about 19,000 homemakers working in the 540 agencies believed to be in operation, compared with the 121 agencies in 1969. However, less than a third of the homemakers reported in this survey worked full time. Assuming that one full-time homemaker is equivalent to two part-time workers, this suggests that there were about 12,500 full-time, equivalent (F.T.E.) workers in Canada, or 0.5 F.T.E.'s per 1,000 population (p. 9).

2. Nusberg (1984, 68) noted that the virtual elimination of home visits by physicians is particularly important for the elderly "... because of their reduced mobility and the need to examine how the older patient's social and physical environment may influence his or her health status." In contrast, home visits to older persons are still common in the U.S.S.R., where persons over age fifty account for more than 50% of physicians' home visits. In Britain, two-thirds of persons seventy-five and older obtain medical consultations at home.

3. In the Regional Municipality of Waterloo, Ontario, a survey of three chronic care units or hospitals and eleven nursing homes, found two of the former willing to admit patients as needed for up to four weeks in a calendar year. Two nursing homes provided a total of six vacation-care beds. Use of these beds was generally described as sporadic. In this same Region, four homes for the aged had some arrangements for vacation relief. One institution had two beds designated and had received six individuals in one year (Waterloo Region Social Resources Council and District Health Council 1985).

4. As an illustration, Opit (1977) compared the costs of providing care to two elderly widows, both living alone. One, who had severe dementia and incontinence and had no social contacts, received three and a half hours of nursing care and fifteen hours of home help a week. The other woman was almost blind with cataracts, was frail, deaf and had difficulty walking. She received about fifteen minutes of nursing care a week and three hours of home help but had daily visits from her neighbours. Opit estimated that the cost of service for the former case was about five times that of the latter.

5. Nusberg (1984, 129) quotes a study which suggests that lower institutionalization rates in Bristol, England, compared with Stockholm, Sweden, where there are extensive community services, may be due in part to the fact that more women work in Stockholm and thus are less available to provide support for elderly relatives.

CHAPTER 5

HEALTH STATUS AND THERAPEUTIC PROGRAMS

Chapter 3 provided data about the age and sex of residents of long-term care institutions across Canada, showing the preponderance of the elderly and particularly the very old – those over age eighty-five. Section 3.2 discussed some of the factors associated with institutional admission, such as confusion, difficulties with one or more of the activities of daily living, bowel or bladder incontinence, and the presence of two or more chronic diseases. The role of social factors such as living arrangements and family income were also mentioned. This chapter provides further information about the health status of residents and will discuss some of the programs available in long-term care facilities.

5.1 PROFILE OF RESIDENTS AND PHILOSOPHY OF CARE

There are few national data about the characteristics of residents of long-term care facilities except for age, sex, and average length of stay (see Chapter 3). For more information about their physical and mental health, functional abilities, and social background, it is necessary to turn to studies of small population groups. These may involve individuals already living in an institution or applicants for long-term care. For example, data concerning applicants to the Hamilton-Wentworth Placement Co-ordination Service (PCS) can be examined. Even in the 1970s, nearly 75% of those for whom nursing home care was recommended were aged seventy-five years and older, and over one third were eighty-five and older (Reizenstein 1977). More recent statistics are similar (Hamilton-Wentworth Placement Co-ordination Service 1985). Not surprisingly in view of the age of the applicants, females outnumbered males by almost two to one. As another example, Table 5.1 gives the age-sex distribution of the elderly in long-term care from a survey in Saskatchewan.

As mentioned in Section 3.2, applicants to and residents of long-term care facilities are likely to have one or more chronic health problems and these conditions impair the individual's ability for self-care in one or more ways. Among the major types of physical impairment that affect elderly residents of nursing homes are circulatory disorders such as heart disease and stroke;

61

TABLE 5.1

AGE/SEX DISTRIBUTION OF THE ELDERLY
IN LONG-TERM CARE IN SASKATCHEWAN;
PERCENTAGES (N = 948: WEIGHTED)

	Age Group			
Sex	65 to 74	75 to 84	85 Plus	65+
Male	16.6	34.7	48.7	100
Female	9.3	34.2	56.5	100
Total	11.6	34.4	54.0	100

SOURCE: Stolee et al. 1981, p. 21. Reproduced with permission of the authors.

arthritis and other disorders of the skeletal system; and metabolic disorders such as diabetes. Visual and hearing problems are also frequent. However, for the Hamilton-Wentworth PCS applicants for nursing home care, nearly three-quarters had vision at least adequate for personal safety, and a similar proportion had adequate hearing (Reizenstein 1977). Mental disorders are prevalent among the institutionalized elderly and these also affect functional competence (see Section 3.2). Less than 20% of these Hamilton-Wentworth PCS applicants had normal memory and orientation, and about a third suffered from moderate to extreme depression. Table 5.2 indicates the frequency of groups of disease conditions recorded for the PCS applicants during 1984-85.

It is the functional capacity of elderly people which is of central importance in the decision to seek admission to a long-term care facility. Mobility, for example, may be limited by arthritis, a stroke, heart or respiratory conditions. As Kane and Kane (1982, 8) note:

> Functional problems cannot be described adequately by a medical or psychiatric diagnosis. Two persons with the diagnosis of, say, diabetes, stroke, or schizophrenia, may have vastly different functional abilities and therefore long-term care needs.

A review, therefore, of the activities of daily living (ADL) is a major component of the assessment for long-term care (Grant 1985b). The early statistics from the Hamilton-Wentworth PCS for those applicants recommended for nursing home placement, show the extent of problems. Less than 20% of this group required no assistance with ambulation, nearly half were immobile or needed assistance, and the remainder used a cane, crutches or wheelchair. Moreover, this ability to get about was circumscribed, since over half were described as being physically or mentally unable to travel. Related to this is the fact that over 80% were reported to be physically and/or mentally unable to shop. Within the

TABLE 5.2

DIAGNOSES RECORDED FOR APPLICANTS TO HAMILTON-WENTWORTH PLACEMENT CO-ORDINATION SERVICE, 1984–85

Diagnosis	Absolute Frequency	Percentage of 5,710
1. Conditions related to cerebral dysfunction	1,525	26.7
2. Conditions related to cardiac dysfunction	702	12.3
3. Conditions classed as arthritis	370	6.5
4. Hypertension	360	6.3
5. Conditions related to central nervous system	296	5.2
6. Diabetic conditions	293	5.1
7. Conditions related to respiratory dysfunction	271	4.7
8. Neoplastic diseases	222	3.9
9. Hip fractures	153	2.7
	4,192	73.4

Number of diagnoses recorded = 5,710

Average number of diagnoses per referral = 2.5

Number of Referrals = 2,291

SOURCE: Hamilton-Wentworth Placement Co-ordination Service 1985. Reproduced with permission of J. Caygill.

home, nearly 90% of these individuals for whom a nursing home had been recommended, were unable to prepare a meal, and less than 20% could perform light housekeeping tasks. Turning to personal care, a third were unable to bathe themselves, and almost all the others needed some assistance or supervision. About one quarter had to be dressed; nearly 60% needed assistance or supervision. Feeding was less of a problem. Nearly 40% needed to no help, and another 35% only minor assistance. Transferring, for example, from bed to chair, or chair to toilet, caused problems for more than two-thirds.

Urinary incontinence is a major problem among elderly applicants for long-term care. The Hamilton-Wentworth statistics show that 16% of those recommended for nursing home care were incontinent and about another 40% were rarely or occasionally incontinent. Bowel control was less of a problem with fewer than 7% being frequently or totally incontinent and nearly 50% having full bowel control. It should be emphasized that these statistics relate to the time of application and there is no indication whether, with appropriate treatment, improvement might take place. Information for residents of long-term care facilities is similar to the above, although there is variation from study to study in the proportions needing assistance with the activities of daily living. Table 5.3 shows dependency by level of care from a study in Saskatchewan.

TABLE 5.3

DEPENDENCY BY LEVEL OF CARE,[1]
SASKATCHEWAN, 1980, PERCENTAGES

	Level of Care			
Activity[2]	I	II	III	IV
Bathing	43.8	57.0	79.1	94.9
Dressing	3.1	10.6	49.8	89.7
Eating	1.2	3.3	20.9	48.4
Transferring	0.6	4.4	40.7	87.0
Use of Toilet	–	3.9	33.5	85.6
	N = 160	N = 179	N = 230	N = 158

1. Level I: individuals require no more than an average of 20 minutes of supervisory care per day.

   Level II: individuals require no more than an average of 45 minutes of supervisory and personal care per day.

   Level III: individuals require an average of two hours of personal and basic nursing care per day.

   Level IV: for long-term restorative or palliative care. All persons at this level require care on a 24-hour basis.

2. Needs at least occasional assistance.

Source: Stolee et al. 1981, pp. 13–14, 31. Reproduced with permission of the authors.

The goal of geriatric medicine is to maintain the independence of elderly patients. This can still apply to residents of long-term care facilities, within the limits of their disabilities. However, there must be a willingness to accept some risk with this independence (see Section 5.4.3). Reichel (1983, 1–10) has listed ten essential aspects in the care of the elderly, and all of these have relevance to the institutionalized. Reichel's important concepts, representing a holistic approach, are: compassion and humanism; continuity of care; bolstering the family and home (the family continues to have a place in the resident's life); communication skills; doctor-patient relationship (which can be expanded to a consideration of staff-resident relationships); need for thorough evaluation and assessment; prevention and health maintenance; intelligent treatment; interdisciplinary collaboration; and respect for the usefulness and value of the aged individual. Brody (1977a, 140–41) has said that long-term care facilities must reject a custodial approach in favour "of a positive philosophy of active treatment and rehabilitation" (see also Section 6.3). The interrelated and mutually dependent services needed for the elderly are: maintenance services, such as shelter, food and safety, to preserve biological life; health services to maintain maximum health and functional capacities; personal care; and psychosocial services. These services must provide not only survival and treatment of disease, but also stimulation, dignity and enjoyment.

5.2 MEDICAL ASPECTS

This is not the place for a detailed discussion of medical conditions associated with the elderly since these can be found in standard texts of geriatric medicine (see, for example, Brocklehurst 1985; Reichel 1983; Anderson and Williams 1983). Instead, this section will review some conditions, common among the elderly, which are of particular relevance to long-stay residents of institutions. These conditions may precipitate or be associated with the need for admission to a long-term care facility, and/or they may affect the care required. Certain topics are discussed elsewhere – urinary incontinence in Section 5.3, osteoporosis and falls in Section 5.4, psychogeriatric programs in Section 5.5 and the impact of medications in Section 6.5.

Many physical changes common to old age require particular care and attention from the nursing and other staff of the institution or affect what the individual can do. The wrinkled, dry skin of the elderly is often associated with itching, and this may be severe enough to cause loss of sleep and damage to the skin from scratching. The importance of monitoring elderly residents, particularly those who are immobile, for early signs of pressure sores, is well known. Poor vision results from a number of changes. Presbyopia, or a diminishing ability of the lens to focus for near vision, is the commonest cause, but cataract, degeneration of the retina, and glaucoma are of more serious significance, since there is the potential for total loss of vision. Failing vision often results in falls, spills and breakages due to misjudgement, and frustration as the ability to read, do craft work or other activities is reduced. Poor vision may both seriously affect the ability to remain independent and be associated with confusion in a new or altered environment.

In the musculoskeletal system, a slow atrophy of muscles occurs with aging, and these tend to be replaced by fatty tissue. As lean body mass, composed of the muscles, liver, brain and kidneys, decreases, the individual requires less food energy and smaller drug doses. Failure to take account of these changes may result not only in obesity, perhaps with associated hypertension or diabetes, but in a variety of potentially serious problems because of drug overdosage (see Sections 5.4.2 and 6.5). In addition to fractures of the femoral neck and of the wrist associated with falls, osteoporosis of vertebral bodies may result in compression fractures and partial collapse. The latter, with disc degeneration, leads to loss of height and bowed back. While calcium is lost from bone, cartilages and ligaments tend to become calcified. Changes such as these within the rib cage can reduce respiratory efficiency, and thus may limit the person's activity.

In addition to these aging changes, there is a progressive decline in the function of major internal systems – metabolism, circulation, elimination and homeostatic control. There are a number of implications for the care of the institutionalized elderly. Problems occur with eating because of reduced salivation and the poor state of the teeth or dentures. Recognition of these problems is necessary to ensure adequate and palatable nutrition. There appears to be an increased incidence of diabetes mellitus in older age groups, but an elderly person with higher than normal blood sugar levels should be evaluated carefully, since too hasty treatment may result in hypoglycemia and the risk of permanent cerebral damage (Cape 1978, 25–29).

Poor blood circulation is a cause of many problems in the elderly, and good foot care, for example, is particularly important for those with a reduced blood supply. Heart disease is the most common cause of death for males and females over age sixty-five, but the activities of an old person with an aged but not diseased heart need not be seriously curtailed, since homeostatic mechanisms generally act to protect vital organs. However, one aspect of aging is the impairment of physiological systems which preserve homeostasis, with the result that the body is less able to adapt and more subject to environmental stresses. Deterioration in the function of the nervous system, kidneys, lungs, etc., lead to difficulty in the control, for example, of body temperature, water and electrolyte balance and blood pressure. Hypothermia and dehydration, therefore, are more likely to occur among the elderly. Concern about these risks may be a component in the decision to admit an individual, and nursing staff should also be aware of the possibility of dehydration among residents.

Among the clinical conditions which are common in the elderly, cerebrovascular accident (stroke) ranks as a major cause of morbidity and mortality. It produces a varying degree of disability in a high proportion of those affected, and often deprives the individual of independence and a feeling of self-worth. The impact, therefore, on the elderly person and on the the family is considerable. Long-term management of the stroke patient has, as its goal, restoration of independence and self-sufficiency, bearing in mind the physical illness, the resulting disabilities, the commonly associated depression and fear, and the social conditions of the patient. Assessment and the start of rehabilitation through programs such as physical, occupational and speech therapy may be carried out in the acute-care setting but, for the individual returning to or being admitted to long-term care, it is usually important to continue rehabilitation (see also Section 5.6).

Arthritis in its various forms is a major cause of disability among the elderly (Grob 1983, 344–59). Osteoarthritis affects mainly the weight-bearing joints (knees, hips, lumbar spine), the cervical spine, and terminal joints of the fingers. Pain, stiffness and eventual deformity occur. Rheumatoid arthritis involves the small joints of the hands and feet, although other joints may also be attacked. Most elderly patients with rheumatoid arthritis have the residuals of this disease, which may have left them with severe deformity of the hands and wrists. Involvement of hips and knees, and associated muscle weakness may seriously impair their ability to get about. Limitation of movement, which may affect the ability to shop, move about the house, cook or provide self-care, are common problems associated with the need for institutionalization, and can limit the individual within the residential facility. In the long-term care setting, treatment is likely to be limited to maintenance of joint movement, exercises to strengthen muscle groups, and instruction in the use of aids to daily living.

When considering the health of the elderly, certain points should be noted. The need for repeated, regular reassessment must be emphasized, since important adverse changes may occur gradually and not be immediately obvious. Moreover, disease may present in unusual ways. Symptoms and signs common in younger patients may be absent or altered in the old. The elderly are also likely to have multiple acute and/or chronic conditions. Related to this is the "iceberg phenomenon," where only the tip of the total medical picture is apparent. That is, the extent of illness present is often greater than the physician is aware of, since the elderly may not complain about problems which they ascribe to "old age" (Williamson et al. 1964).

5.3 URINARY INCONTINENCE

As already noted in Sections 3.2 and 5.1, an important problem among the elderly, particularly those resident in long-term care institutions, is urinary incontinence. Estimates of its prevalence among elderly people living in the community range from less than 2% to over 40% (Milne 1976), depending on the definition of the condition, the population studied and the methods used (see for example, McGrother et al. 1986; Thomas et al. 1980; Vetter et al. 1981; Yarnell et al. 1982; Yarnell and St. Leger 1979). Among the institutionalized elderly approximately 50% are affected by urinary dysfunction, including incontinence (Jewett et al. 1981; Ouslander et al. 1982).

This condition represents a major medical, psychological and social problem and it is often a cause of dependency. The medical consequences of incontinence include urinary infections, pressure sores, perineal rashes, and falls. The psychosocial consequences are embarrassment, isolation, depression and increased likelihood of institutionlization. It is the latter which contributes to the economic costs of institutional care (Resnick and Yalla 1985). Medical texts (e.g., Anderson and Williams 1983; Brocklehurst 1985), specialized books (e.g., Brocklehurst 1984; Mandelstam 1980; Willington 1976), and review articles (e.g., Resnick and Yalla 1985) can be approached for the types and causes of urinary incontinence and the range of therapies available. However, certain points relevant to the care of the institutionalized elderly are worth emphasizing.

It should be remembered that urinary incontinence is only a symptom, and the possible causes of the condition are numerous. It may be classified as transient (see Table 5.4) or established, and proper evaluation of the patient is important. Unfortunately, incontinence is often attributed to aging and not investigated further, particularly when there is a gradual onset and progression. Aging changes may affect the lower urinary tract,

TABLE 5.4

COMMON CAUSES OF TRANSIENT INCONTINENCE

Delirium or confusional state
Urinary infection
Atrophic urethritis or vaginitis
Drugs, e.g., sedatives, antiparkinsonian agents
Psychological disorders, especially depression
Endocrine disorders, e.g., hyperglycemia
Restricted mobility
Stool impaction

Adapted from: Resnick and Yalla 1985. Reprinted by permission of *The New England Journal of Medicine.*

and may predispose the individual to incontinence, but these changes alone do not precipitate incontinence. This predisposition, and the increased likelihood that an elderly person will experience additional pathological, physiological, or pharmacological insults, underlie the higher incidence of incontinence in the elderly. It is not an inevitable consequence of aging, but a pathological condition that usually can be improved or cured (Resnick and Yalla 1985).

For the staff caring for elderly residents, it is important to remember that the patient must be treated as a "whole" person with attention directed to the social and psychological problem as well as to the medical problem. Apart from specific therapies relevant to the physical cause of incontinence, symptomatic treatment can be of help. Ensuring that a bedside commode or urinal is easily accessible, that the bed is low enough for the resident to get out of safely, that washrooms are identified clearly, are well lit, and provide adequate grab-bars, are some of the aspects of "designing towards continence" (Hood 1976). Staff should understand the feelings of confusion, anxiety and depression that may follow institutional admission, and which may be associated with temporary incontinence. Patience towards those who are deaf, aphasic or clumsy is needed. Other simple procedures such as regular toileting, restricting fluids in the evening, maintaining physical activity, limiting the use of drugs to induce sleep, and provision of privacy are all helpful. Habit retraining, bladder-sphincter biofeedback, and pelvic floor exercises (Burgio et al. 1985; Resnick and Yalla 1985) are some of the techniques used in addition to symptomatic measures. In some cases, surgery may be appropriate. Drugs may have a place in therapy but many have side effects (Anderson and Williams 1983, 176–78), or their efficacy is not proven (Resnick and Yalla 1985). Remembering the transient nature of the condition in many patients, an overall success rate of about 50% may be achieved using a combination of therapies, accompanied by a positive, supportive attitude on the part of staff to encourage independence and continence, rather than assuming the opposite. However, a major factor governing success is the mental state of the patient (Anderson and Williams 1983, 177).

5.4 FALLS AMONG THE ELDERLY

The tendency for the elderly to fall is a major problem and a matter of concern because of the potential for serious injury, restriction of mobility and loss of independence. Even the fear of falling may affect independence through a loss of confidence in the ability to get about safely. Concern over the risk of falls is often a contributing reason for the admission of elderly people to a residential facility.

5.4.1 The Incidence of Falls

The elderly have a relatively high number of reported falls and these falls are more likely to be fatal. In Canada, those sixty-five and older account for more than 70% of deaths due to falls (Berry et al. 1981). These statistics, however, do not indicate the total incidence of falls and neglect those deaths in which the interval between the fall and death obscures a causal relationship (Gryfe et al. 1977). Establishing prevalence rates for falls is made difficult by the problems associated with reporting falls accurately. Many studies, for example, have been retrospective, and the reporting of symptoms by the elderly may be unreliable (Milne et al. 1970). Reports may also be confused by the failure to distinguish between accidents and falls, although it is commonly stated that most of the accidents occurring within institutions, result from falls (e.g., Pablo 1977a). Moreover, if neither the population at risk nor the duration of observation are defined clearly, rates of falling cannot be calculated. This is particularly important in examining falls among the elderly since their likelihood of a prolonged stay in a hospital or long-term care institution is greater and therefore this increases the period of risk and the number of falls which may be experienced. Studies have reported a fall rate of 42.7 per 10,000 patient days and 836 per 1,000 persons per year (Berry et al. 1981; Holliday et al. 1985), while in a study of a relatively independent elderly institutional population, Gryfe et al. (1977) reported an overall rate of 668 falls per 1,000 per year.

Gryfe et al. (1977) noted that the rate of falling in institutions rose with age after the age of seventy-five, but that there was a relatively high rate among the youngest group, those less than seventy-five. This may be due to an unusual amount of physical, emotional, and social disability, reflected in the relatively early age at which these individuals were institutionalized. However others, in discussing falls among hospital patients and residents of long-term care facilities, have suggested that younger, fitter individuals may be more likely to be mobile and more likely to resist the limitations imposed on them by their physical condition, and therefore to have more opportunity to fall. It has also been found that the proportion of falls and other accidents is significantly greater on the assessment and rehabilitation wards than on other wards (Berry et al. 1981; Pablo 1977a). Studies have varied in the frequency with which men and women are reported to fall, and their fall rates (Catchen 1983; Sehested and Severin-Nielsen 1977). So far as institutionalized populations are concerned, one wonders whether the reported figures for falls by men and women have been adjusted for the usually larger proportion of female residents.

Another factor regarding the opportunity to fall is the time of day and therefore the activities associated with the fall. Several studies have reported the highest rate of incidents during the day shift (Berry et al. 1981; Pablo 1977a; Sehested and Severin-Nielsen 1977), when residents are likely to be involved in physiotherapy, occupational therapy, recreation and social activities as well as various activities of daily living and nursing care. Contrary to suggestions that accidents, including falls, are more common when staff numbers are low (Catchen 1983; Walshe and Rosen 1979), these higher daytime fall rates emphasize the importance of opportunity to the risk of falling and the fact that the presence of staff does not guarantee safety from falls.

Some investigators, however, report an increased number of falls during the evening and night shifts (Walshe and Rosen 1979), which they attribute to individuals needing to use the toilet, and associated factors such as sleepiness, climbing out of bed, poor lighting and possible disorientation. At whatever time of day, falls are more likely to occur during the first week after admission when the person is unfamiliar with his or her surroundings (Catchen 1983; Sehested and Severin-Nielsen 1977; Walshe and Rosen 1979). The majority of falls occur in the resident's room, particularly at the bedside, or in the washroom (Ashley et al. 1977; Berry et al. 1981; Pablo 1977a).

Many studies (e.g., Pablo 1977a; Sehested and Severin-Nielsen 1977) have found that accidents are often not isolated incidents but rather that two, three or more falls per individual are reported. One such study (Catchen 1983) at an acute care hospital noted that "repeaters" tended to be male and to have been in hospital longer. Organic mental syndrome or stroke was the primary diagnosis listed on 40% of all repeater accident reports. Both conditions may produce periods of disorientation and decreased muscular co-ordination. It was also suggested that those who fell more than once tended to be strong-willed determined individuals who were unable to accept their current physical and/or mental impairment.

The majority of falls do not result in severe injury (Catchen 1983). In one study (Gryfe et al. 1977), over 80% of the residents who fell were not injured or received only trivial injury. The incidence of fractures among those who fell in different studies of long-term care facilities was 3.2% (Berry et al. 1981), 4% (Sehested and Severin-Nielsen 1977) and 6% (Gryfe et al. 1977). Even though the proportion of falls causing severe injury may be small, this remains a serious problem in the care of the elderly. A seemingly minor injury in a debilitated patient may cause considerable discomfort and eventually a serious outcome.

5.4.2 Precipitating Factors Associated with Falls

The aetiology of falls usually involves an interaction between factors inherent in the "faller," intrinsic causes, and factors circumstantial to the faller, extrinsic causes (Ashley et al. 1977). The relative importance of different factors is not clear, but the importance of extrinsic factors has been stressed, since these are frequently the most readily identifiable and potentially modifiable aspects. Nevertheless, falls due solely to extrinsic causes are less common than those due to intrinsic factors (Gryfe 1983).

Postural control is achieved by a complex series of messages to the brain from the skin, muscles, joints, ears and eyes. These messages are then translated into appropriate responses to maintain balance. Age-related physiological changes may affect this system. Impaired eyesight and changes in the labyrinth of the inner ear often cause body-orienting reflexes to become less effective with age. Muscle strength is reduced, reaction times are prolonged, foot problems and arthritic changes in the hips and knees make walking awkward and even painful. In such circumstances an obstacle or change in the terrain may provoke a stumble for which the individual cannot compensate quickly. A variety of age-related changes can affect the blood supply to the brain. This may explain sudden "drop attacks," which are associated with no loss of consciousness or other symptoms (Cape 1978, 120–21). In other cases, less efficient physiological control mechanisms result in postural hypotension, in which a sudden drop in blood pressure occurs when the person stands up. This may be followed by dizziness and a fall.

Elderly people experience a variety of clinical conditions which can increase the risk of falling. Cardiac arrhythmias are believed to be an important cause of falls, while diseases of the neurological system, such as Parkinson's disease and cerebrovascular disease, may be implicated. Senile epilepsy, sometimes resulting from a previous cerebrovascular accident but often with no obvious cause, may result in transient loss of consciousness without signs of convulsion or incontinence. Dizziness, a common but vague complaint among the elderly, can be due to Ménière's disease, to ear infection, or to injury in the past (Gordon 1982). A fall may be precipitated by confusion, the causes of which are many and varied (see Cape 1978, 92, 100). These include infections, cardiovascular, cerebrovascular and metabolic conditions, drug effects, psychosocial depression and primary dementing conditions such as Alzheimer's disease.

Falls, therefore, may indicate a serious underlying illness and should be taken seriously even when minor. Gryfe (1983) states that a patient who has had at least three falls in the past year should be regarded as demonstrating evidence of underlying disease. These falls tend to have a regular pattern, such as the patient who repeatedly injures the same side of the body, or has repeated head injuries, suggesting failure of normal protective reflexes.

Many medications can have side effects which increase the risk of falling. Antihypertensives, antidepressants, diuretics, hypnotics and tranquilizers may lead to postural hypotension. Hypoglycemia and faintness may result from inadequate control over antidiabetic agents, and certain antibiotics can cause or aggravate disease (Gordon 1982). Diuretics increase the tendency for elderly people to experience frequency and urgency of urination, and aspirin may result in a fall by inducing gastrointestinal bleeding.

Although only a small percentage of falls among elderly institutionalized persons result in fractures (see Section 5.4.1), the chance of a fracture occurring is increased by the presence of osteoporosis, a condition involving a progressive reduction in bone mass with increasing age. A number of writers have linked an increase in fractures of the neck of the femur in older women with the presence of osteoporosis. These fractures are associated with considerable morbidity and mortality. It has been estimated that, in the United States, 40,000 hip-fracture patients per year may need long-term care because of resulting permanent disability (Wingate 1984). Unfortunately, lack of exercise and prolonged bed rest are believed to aggravate the condition of osteoporosis (Anderson and Williams 1983, 250). A variety of treatments have been advocated including estrogen replacement therapy, calcium supplements and vitamin D. However, the short- and long-term benefits have not been established (Doepel 1985).

Among environmental factors, use of the wheelchair has been reported as a potential hazard, with falls resulting from the failure to keep the seatbelt fastened or to apply the brakes (Berry et al. 1981; Catchen 1983; Pablo 1977a). The problem of unstable or rolling furniture also applies to beds, bed tables, bedside cupboards and chairs, any of which may be used by the elderly for support. Bedside rails, intended to protect the individual from falling out of bed, may cause a more serious fall if a confused and determined person tries to climb over them. Short side rails are believed to be more appropriate for many individuals, since they will act as a reminder of the edge of the bed yet can be a support rather than a hindrance in getting out of bed (Price 1965). In general, restraints are not an appropriate way to prevent falls (Cape 1978, 97; Snyder et al. 1978). The disturbing effect which bed rails, body holders, wrist straps and other restraints have on patients, in many cases defeats their purpose, and also is contrary to the overall goal of establishing a comfortable environment. Use of medications to provide "chemical restraint" is equally undesirable.

Not only concern for the individual's safety, but also the risk of litigation in the event of a fall may explain the tendency to sedate some residents, but these reasons rarely justify such restriction of the individual (Mitchell-Pedersen et al. 1985; Schafer 1985; but see also, Grauer 1985; Hoaken 1985), nor do the risk of drug side-effects (see also Section 6.5). Reducing the use of restraints seems to have positive repercussions for the staff as well as the residents. In one geriatric unit where a 97% reduction in the use of physical restraints was achieved over one year, ... "Staff became highly creative in looking after patients without the use of restraints and feelings of pride developed as they were able to provide care that honoured the autonomy of their patients." (Mitchell-Pedersen et al. 1985).

The frequency with which falls occur in the bathroom emphasizes the importance of providing appropriate grab-bars, vertically placed as well as horizontally. Handrails elsewhere may be inadequate if the hand cannot grip them fully (Holliday et al. 1985). Falls also occur because of cluttered rooms and corridors, trailing wires, unsuitable footwear, slippery and over-shiny floors which, by causing glare in the sunshine, may dazzle. Conversely, poor night vision and a need for increased illumination make adequate lighting, particularly at night and at floor level, essential. Other problems include low, poorly designed chairs, beds which are too high, and a lack of colour contrasts in corridors and rooms.

5.4.3 Preventive Measures

Although it is not possible to prevent all falls, it is possible to reduce their number and severity. It is important to assess each patient's risk of falling, and to re-evaluate this periodically. Consideration should be given to sensory and other deficits of aging, the presence of acute and chronic diseases, medications, mental state and personality, bowel and bladder habits, and any past history of falls. Careful observation of elderly individuals is desirable, particularly in the first week after admission, and identifying the beds of high-risk individuals is recommended.

Staff education is an important component of any program to reduce the number of falls among the elderly in health-care facilities. An understanding of physiological changes because of aging, the potential for falls associated with many medical conditions and the effect of medications are all necessary for a comprehensive risk assessment. The program should promote awareness among the staff of the environmental risks, and the administration should be aware of the part played by furniture design, by the decoration of the institution and other features such as lights, floor coverings, handrails and grab-bars (Clarke-Williams 1983, 71–89). Although lack of supervision is not usually considered to be an important cause of falls (Sehested and Severin-Nielsen 1977), staffing patterns may need to be reviewed, and television cameras or photo-electric alert systems may facilitate observation of high-risk patients. Nursing procedures which may be related to falls should be discussed and the need for good communication between staff, particularly when shifts change, should be emphasized. Wherever possible nursing procedures and rounds should be planned to meet patient rather than staff needs, so that, for example, patients are not kept waiting for bedpans or assistance with dressing. It is recognized that this is not easy, but awareness of the aging individual's difficulties, and a willingness to allow flexibility in nursing and other procedures, may go a long way towards achieving this desirable situation.

Patients also need to receive instruction and reminders about the potential for and risks of falling. All new residents should receive an orientation to their new surroundings on admission. Careful and repeated instruction about transfers, use of assistive devices, the need to change position slowly and to wear non-slip footwear should be part of a rehabilitation program. Several authors have emphasized the need to restrict the indiscriminate use of wheelchairs and to encourage walking with other assistive devices such as a cane or walker (Barbieri 1983). The lower incidence of falls among patients with arthritis, fractures and amputations (Sehested and Severin-Nielsen 1977) has been attributed to a program of movement therapy.

Finally, it should be emphasized that the risk of falls should not be considered a reason to restrict mobilization and rehabilitation of elderly patients, nor is it necessarily a justification for institutionalization. Immobility has its own risks, and the need for an individual's independence and privacy makes it necessary to accept some risks, including the possibility of falls.

5.5 PSYCHOGERIATRIC PROGRAMS

Old people suffer from the psychiatric illnesses occurring in adults of all age groups. They also experience psychiatric problems peculiar to old age, and related to the perception of old age in our culture (Comfort 1980, 1). A nonspecific combination of physical and mental symptoms may be the presenting features of a wide range of medical conditions, many of them remediable and some of them therapeutically induced, that is, iatrogenic. Disorientation and confusion, for example, are relatively easily induced in the elderly by infection, medications, and electrolyte imbalance. In addition, there has been the attitude that mental decline and illness is normal in the old. The prospect of becoming "senile" is a common fear and results in apprehension when lapses of memory or brief episodes of confusion occur. In fact, chronic brain syndrome is neither an inevitable concomitant of old age nor the commonest major psychiatric disorder. Rather, depression is the most common problem.

However, as indicated in Section 5.1, the dementias and other psychological problems are common among the institutionalized elderly. Moreover, the prevalence of dementia has increased and probably will continue to do so as the population ages. At present, families frequently look after confused elderly relatives. Improved community services provide assistance, and increasing attention and support is being given to those caring for individuals affected by Alzheimer's disease or other dementing conditions. In the future, however, families may not be able to provide this care as more women work and a rising divorce rate disrupts many families. The result is likely to be that more of the confused elderly will need institutional care (see also Section 7.4.1). Peace (1984, 90) has also pointed out that:

> ... misdiagnosis of both functional mental illness, such as depression, and organic mental illness, such as acute brain syndrome or chronic brain failure, ... can lead to inappropriate admission to residential facilities.

Unfortunately, the emphasis in long-term care facilities has traditionally been on custodial care or drug therapies. This is not surprising considering the lack of geriatric mental health training for staff in general, and the scarcity of specialists such as psychogeriatricians and psychiatric nurses. There has also been a therapeutic nihilism based on the concept that "all of the aged had incurable brain damage" (Eisdorfer 1977, 65). A diagnosis of dementia tended to induce a feeling in staff that nothing could be achieved, and therefore little was done to involve the resident. Such lack of stimulation, often accentuated by sensory losses such as poor vision or hearing, led to even greater confusion. The dementias probably represent the most important single drain on community health resources, but the prevention of iatrogenic dementias and those aggravated or induced by lack of activity and stimulation could ease the situation.

Progress is being made with a number of behavioural, interpersonal, environmental and biological approaches (Comfort 1980, 56–57; Council on Scientific Affairs 1986) and with the training and support of both families and staff (Arie 1977, 75–77; Ontario Association of Homes for the Aged 1985). The implications of architectural design are being considered, and various models for the provision of psychogeriatric services have been proposed (see for example, Comfort 1980, 87–92; Jolley et al. 1982, 149–65; Simon 1984). Sutcliffe (1983, 189–90) has emphasized the importance of co-ordination between staff, and the need for a multidisciplinary team to assess and reassess patients on a planned and regular basis. In this way, slow progress or deterioration can be detected and realistic goals set for each individual. Careful monitoring can also help to convince staff that it is possible to maintain and sometimes to improve patients' functional capabilities.

5.5.1 Specific Treatment Approaches

One technique used in the care of confused and disoriented elderly residents of long-term care facilities is reality orientation (Comfort 1980, 56; Edelson and Lyons 1985, 50–76). The primary purpose of reality orientation for these individuals is not as a treatment that aims to improve memory and other features of cognitive performance. Rather this technique is a basic method of communication with the resident by all staff. The technique uses a process of day-to-day information exchange between staff and resident that aims to stimulate and develop the senses and to increase social contacts. This provides support to the individual's failing memory, and a feeling of comfort and security to the confused. A sense of security, a steady supportive relationship with staff and a reduction in the level of anxiety may also have a beneficial effect on memory and behaviour.

Aspects of the facility itself can be utilized to counteract residents' confusion and failing memory. Environmental methods to assist orientation include painting doors different colours, placing a large clock and calendar in each room, and using name badges with large print. Sensory deficits such as deafness and poor vision should be corrected as far as possible.

In addition to the incorporation of reality orientation in day-to-day contact between staff and residents, it may also be used in small group classes (Sutcliffe 1983, 192–95). These and other activity programs (see Section 5.6) help to provide important social contacts and sensory stimulation. This does not mean constant activity but social involvement with staff, volunteers and other residents, and the repetition of information such as the date, place, people's names and current news. For most confused residents the goal is to provide:

> (a) a means of reinforcing reality, (b) a satisfying social experience, and (c) a means of stimulating residual cognitive abilities. (Edelson and Lyons 1985, 66)

Imperceptible improvements may occur, but the process must be continuous and consistent. Such classes are valuable in helping staff to understand each resident's mental functioning and in improving staff attitudes. Understanding what lies behind a resident's anxiety, disruptive behaviour or wandering may also help staff to develop creative ways to handle such situations (Mitchell-Pedersen et al. 1985).

Feil (1982, 2) believes that there are some disoriented elderly people who have "outlived their ability to defend themselves against losses and stay oriented." For these people reality orientation is not appropriate and, indeed, may lead to increased confusion, hostility and withdrawal. Instead these individuals return to the past to survive and use early learned emotional memories to replace intellectual thinking. To help such people, Feil developed the "Validation" method in the 1960s and 1970s. The method uses empathy to "tune into" the disoriented person and thus to pick up clues with which the therapist can help to put the resident's feelings into words. Although not all patients respond, particularly younger old people with severe brain damage, Feil believes that the system builds trust, feelings of safety and strength and, from that, a sense of worth (see also Coons 1983, 149).

Verwoerdt (1981, 118) considers that psychotherapy with the elderly is not conducted often enough when compared with the apparent need. Treatment efforts can be grouped into three main categories depending on whether therapy is aimed at adjusting the "input" – for example, the stress caused by bereavement; at readjusting the "throughput" – the defence mechanisms used to deal with the stress and associated distress; or at modifying the "output" – the psychological and behavioural responses associated with the defences and coping behaviour. Verwoerdt believes that a selection of treatments is usually necessary. Difficulties arise, however, in applying psychotherapy to patients with dementia, since the medium for transmitting information, the communicative channels, is impaired. In such cases behaviour modification techniques may be successful.

Behaviour modification aims to change unwanted behaviours rather than alter personality. There are four major types of such techniques; positive reinforcement, desensitization, aversive procedures, and modeling. Of these, positive reinforcement is most widely used in long-term care institutions (Brody 1977a, 287). It uses stimulation and reward to produce improvements in personal appearance, hygiene, conversation, punctuality and independence. However, as with other therapies, behaviour modification requires training and commitment on the part of the staff.

Counselling and group work are other programs used with the disturbed elderly. A common experience accompanying old age is the death of spouse, relatives and friends, and this may have a profound effect on a resident's mood and behaviour. Grief and loneliness are important aspects of old age. Bereavement counselling provides an opportunity for the individual to express the feelings of shock, disbelief and anger common to such loss, and then allows the counsellor to assist in handling those feelings. Since old age is a time of many personal losses, such as loss of home, work and independence, individual and group sessions also provide an opportunity to explore the effect of those losses and to bolster self-esteem.

There are difficulties in accurately estimating the incidence of true depressive episodes, which differ qualitatively from grief, because of problems with definitions and diagnoses. Depression is believed to be a problem for a significant minority of older persons. However, although major stresses such as illness or the death of a spouse are more common in old age, the precipitation of depressive illness by major stress is no more common among the elderly than among younger adults (Post 1978). Depression in the old may present in many ways and is commonly undiagnosed. It may present as pseudodementia or confusion, but conversely dementia may be accompanied by depression. The importance of accurate diagnosis lies in the fact that, in the majority of cases, depression is treatable, whereas dementia due to one of the progressive and irreversible processes such as Alzheimer's disease is not, although, as mentioned above, there are ways to assist the disoriented resident.

Other programs of use for individuals who are confused and demented are respite and short-stay beds, day hospitals and day centres (see Section 4.3); the latter are sometimes established specifically for psychogeriatric cases. These programs are available in Canada, though not generally associated with long-term care facilities, and they tend to be available only in large cities. Each of these programs provide care and stimulation for the elderly individual and relief for relatives. However, there is still limited public awareness of their effectiveness. Home-care programs find that clients with senile dementia are the most difficult to manage at home (Kane and Kane 1985a, 218), but earlier referrals to home care, with earlier relief, might delay institutional placement. In areas without separate provision for the elderly with psychiatric illness, the nursing home and extended care or chronic care hospital will be required increasingly for those with chronic brain failure. In Saskatchewan, approximately 70% of patients in extended care hospitals exhibit this condition, and in nursing homes the prevalance varies between 30% and 50% depending on the facility's admission policies (Robertson 1982, 213–14). Little impact will be made on the high rate of institutionalization without providing appropriate support to the care-givers.

Another program, linking community and institution, is the community psychogeriatric service where typically one or more clinical nurse specialists, with training in psychiatric/community mental health nursing, provide consultation and education to nurses working in the community. When requested, the nurse specialists provide a psychiatric assessment of a client and recommendations for management. For nurses and aides working with the elderly in institutions, they provide psychogeriatric seminars and assist in planning programs to help maintain the residents' mental health. As mentioned earlier in this section, emphasis is placed on the need to regard lack of deterioration in a resident's condition as a sign of success, and "to build upon patients' remaining strengths rather than focus on the deficiencies" (Peace 1984, 101).

5.6 REHABILITATIVE, RECREATIONAL AND OTHER PROGRAMS

The various programs and services provided in long-term care facilities can be divided into two groups, those which provide for the physical needs of the resident, and those which minister to psychosocial needs. The former group includes medical and nursing care, and the administrative, dietary, housekeeping and general maintenance functions of the institution. These latter aspects of long-term care facilities do not differ appreciably from those of other health-care institutions and will not be discussed. This section will consider some of the programs which cater to the rehabilitative, psychological and social needs of the elderly residents.

In the past, attention was concentrated on the physical aspects of care for the institutionalized elderly, while rehabilitation, and social and recreational activities were ignored or regarded as "frills." Now, the importance of these programs in providing stimulation, socialization and rehabilitation is recognized. The objectives are extensive and the range of programs which might be provided is large, but in practice those offered are usually limited and affected by the abilities of the residents.

Professionals who may be involved in these various programs include physical and occupational therapists, speech therapists, recreationists and music therapists. However, often they are found only in large long-term care centres. At best, most nursing homes and homes for the aged have to depend on an "activity director," assisted by other staff and volunteers. Not infrequently, therapists complain that their expertise is inadequately or inappropriately used, as other staff do not understand the therapist's function, or are unwilling to co-operate. Edelson and Lyons (1985, 89), however, point to the difficulties experienced by nursing staff not only in preparing residents for an activity program but also in handling some of the mentally impaired who, on return to the ward, are agitated, stubborn and abusive. They suggest that nursing staff generally want residents to be involved, but they disagree about the benefits of programs.

A physical therapy service for long-stay residents has the potential to assist many of those suffering from the residuals of stroke, fractures or arthritis. Although restorative goals must be realistic, considerable functional improvements are possible. An improvement in mobility leads to increased independence, less incontinence and the reduced incidence of pressure sores. A physical therapist is also able to assess the resident's physical abilities and potential. Advice and training for the nursing staff in ways to assist residents can also be provided. Exercise groups not only help to mobilize limbs and strengthen muscles, but also encourage social awareness and contacts.

The function of the occupational therapist is not to keep the resident "occupied," although traditional activities such as basket weaving and other crafts may have therapeutic value. Wolcott (1983, 186) describes occupational therapy techniques as being designed "to increase either range of motion, strength, dexterity, co-ordination or some combination of these elements." The occupational therapist is also responsible for supplying a variety of adaptive devices or aids which residents may need to carry out various activities of daily living, and in training the individual in their use.

The recreational therapist, or recreationist, is a relatively new member of the multidisciplinary and rehabilitation team whose function is also not just to find ways to occupy the time of the resident. The therapist's function is to provide recreational and social activities which promote socialization, provide mental stimulation and physical activity. This includes a range of possible activities (see Emodi 1977, 22, 34). In some centres, residents are encouraged to renew old work skills or learn new ones. Visits from outside groups such as school choirs, community speakers, and representatives of the Humane Society with a selection of pets, provide contacts with the community, as do shopping expeditions and other outings organized for residents. Many facilities now have a Residents' Council with some staff representation. Activities such as drama groups, gardening clubs, singing, instrumental and dancing programs and reminiscence groups have been found to have therapeutic value for a wide range of residents, including the mentally impaired (Edelson and Lyons 1985, 103–7). Music appreciation, art, pottery, and other educational classes have also been tried in a number of settings for long-term residents (see for example, chapters 7 through 9 in Denham 1983). Futhermore, such programs offered in hospice units, have been found to encourage a sense of well-being in the dying patient (Frampton 1986). With all these programs, the intent is to sustain or improve the resident's abilities and to promote a sense of confidence and self-worth which add to the quality of life. Unfortunately, there are many long-term care facilities which make little or no effort to provide recreational activities and outings, physical exercise or entertainment. In general, it is accepted that recreational programs are of value for the resident. However this is, as mentioned above, a new area of therapy, and further research is needed to evaluate the format and the effectiveness of the programs more thoroughly.

So far as rehabilitation in general is concerned, it is believed that there is enough knowledge to support certain basic principles of rehabilitation therapy (Wolcott 1983, 188). There is also evidence (Commonwealth of Australia 1979) that as many as a third of the residents of nursing homes would be better situated in a lower-cost domiciliary setting if they received adequate rehabilitation. However, many questions remain such as: Can patients who will most benefit from therapy be identified? How can the right therapy be chosen? What aids and adaptations are most useful? What sort of training is needed, and could volunteers conduct many of the programs? Until such questions are answered and there is firm evidence that rehabilitation is of measurable value, there will continue to be a tendency to regard these programs with some scepticism (Mulley 1981, 24–25).

5.7 SUMMARY AND CONCLUSIONS

In this chapter the health status and various problems of elderly residents of long-term care facilities are identified and discussed. Inability to carry out activities of daily living, as determined by a functional assessment, is important and is not predicted by a specific diagnosis. Following a discussion of the proportion of elderly individuals who are unable to carry out, or need assistance with, activities of daily living, certain major syndromes that are of particular relevance for the elderly in long-term care facilities are considered. Urinary incontinence is a medical, psychological and social problem which is often a cause of dependency. The tendency for the elderly to fall is a major concern and is discussed in some detail. Confused and disoriented elderly comprise a substantial proportion of the institutionalized elderly, and various programs intended to alleviate the problems arising from these disorders are reviewed. The importance of rehabilitation and the psychosocial needs of elderly residents are stressed, and various rehabilitative, social, educational and recreational programs are mentioned.

The following may be concluded:

1. The aim of caring for the frail elderly in institutions is to maintain the independence of elderly patients within the limits of their disabilities.
2. There are many medical conditions associated with the elderly, including arthritis, strokes, and other physical changes common to old age, which may limit the independence of the elderly and necessitate care. Staff must be alert to the gradual and sometimes unusual presentation of illness among the elderly.
3. Urinary incontinence is not an inevitable consequence of aging and often can be cured or improved. Attention should be directed not only to the medical problem but also to the social and psychological aspects, with a positive attitude which encourages independence and continence.
4. The risk of falls should not be considered a reason for restricting mobility. Assessment of the risk of falling should be carried out when an elderly person is admitted and then be re-evaluated periodically.
5. Approaches to assist the confused and disoriented elderly include reality orientation, behaviour modification and validation. Although improvements may occur, success should be regarded as the prevention of deterioration. Day hospitals and day centres can also be of assistance to such individuals and may assist some to remain in their homes. Support for the caregiver is of importance if institutionalization is to be avoided.
6. Apart from medical and nursing care, the psychosocial care of the institutionalized elderly should be considered. The importance of physical and occupational therapists, speech therapists, recreationists, music therapists and activity directors in providing rehabilitation, socialization and activation is noted. Unfortunately, the majority of facilities are still unable to provide many of these services.

CHAPTER 6

INSTITUTIONALIZATION: SOURCES OF CONCERN

This chapter will identify some of the sources of concern relating to the institutionalization of the elderly, highlighting areas where opportunities exist to bring about changes. Many of these areas involve altering attitudes, which may be needed not only by those who work with the elderly and by those who set policy, but also by the elderly themselves. The chapter also discusses some difficulties associated with research in this area, and some questionable remedies. For example, merely to plead for more funding is not regarded as the most effective course of action, since there are indications that available funds could be used in better ways. Moreover, additional funding may lead to more institutionalization, which may or may not be needed. It is hoped that, by addressing these areas of concern, research will be encouraged that would lead to improvements in the care of the elderly.

6.1 METHODOLOGY AND PROBLEMS IN THE STUDY OF INSTITUTIONAL CARE

The first, and general, area of concern is that many research findings are based on inadequate methodology and many users of such information may not be aware of the limitations of these studies. It is not realistic in a monograph of this type to discuss fully even the main areas of methodology, however, in order to be aware of some of the difficulties which arise, a few points will be stressed. For a better understanding, readers are directed to books on statistics or research methodology where an explanation will be found of the difference between anecdotal evidence, association, and a cause-and-effect relationship, as well as what is required to establish this type of evidence.[1]

In Chapters 2 through 5 various aspects of institutionalization were outlined in what are essentially descriptive terms. However, one should be aware that the data are not always complete and accurate. Data regarding the funding for long-term care in Canada, for example, may be accurate, but do not include the value of volunteer work, nor the value of assistance provided by families.

The data summarized in Chapters 2 through 5 also raise the important questions of whether the various types of institutions, the length of time which individuals spend in them and the care and treatment provided, are appropriate. When comparing the rates of institutionalization in various jurisdictions, differences are observed, and rates for Canada are believed to be relatively high (see Section 3.3). However, there is disagreement about how to compare the rates for different countries, partly because definitions for different types of long-term care services vary. It is likely that the relative provision of institutional and community care in Canada could be altered to achieve better results, both from the point of view of the type of care required by individuals, and cost-effectiveness. Cost-effectiveness represents one, but only one, of the key questions concerning institutionalization of the elderly. Moreover, the appropriateness of care may depend on whether the perspective is that of the individual client, the family or society as a whole. These considerations are addressed in some detail in other sections of this chapter, and in Chapter 7, which discusses future options.

6.1.1 Problems in Data Collection

If one wishes to obtain data for the study of the elderly and institutional care, a number of problems become apparent, as follows:

  (a) In data which are published routinely by Statistics Canada, Health and Welfare Canada, and the provincial Ministries, there is a lack of adequate information on the characteristics of residents, and on admissions to, and discharges from long-term care facilities, although information on costs and on the type of facilities themselves is available.
  (b) Sometimes it is difficult to obtain data for age groups subdivided beyond sixty or sixty-five, and it may be impossible to get data on the population over age eighty-five. Many institutionalized elderly are in this latter age-group. Abridged life tables generally give data up to age eighty-four and then group everybody eight-five and older in one category. Also, the data may be unreliable when age is reported at the time of hospitalization or, after death, by their next of kin (Davies 1985).
  (c) Another problem is that death certificates require information on a single cause of death. It is frequently not possible to think of the problems of the elderly in terms of a single variable, a single physiological deficit, or a single cause of death. In fact, it is not easy to describe the complex conditions that lead to the death of an elderly individual (Davies 1985; Jackson 1983; Kohn 1982).
  (d) It is often not feasible or ethical to carry out a randomized trial in order to evaluate alternatives to institutional care. Hence, it is

necessary to utilize other methods, such as "before and after" comparisons, which include control or comparison groups. The important point is that some control group should be included, allowing comparisons between different methods of treatment, and that care is taken to avoid "contamination" when programs are implemented in a residential setting. For example, if a new recreational program is implemented in a treatment group, contamination can occur if the control group is aware of the program and thus affected by this knowledge.

(e) In carrying out any studies as outlined under (d), it is necessary to have an outcome or end-point variable of institutional care, which can be regarded as the "dependent variable." This is not easy, since outcome measures, such as life satisfaction and perceived health, are not always reliable, although methods which estimate physical, emotional and social health status have been developed and utilized (see Section 7.1).

The methods available to collect data concerning institutional care include comparative studies and case studies. The important methodologies of conducting surveys, and of program evaluation will be discussed briefly in Sections 6.1.2 and 6.1.3.

6.1.2 Survey Methodology

One method of obtaining information on the institutionalized elderly is through the use of census data and related material. Census data provide information about almost every member of the population and consequently would appear to be useful. However, as already noted, in seeking information in some detail about the institutionalized elderly, there are a number of disadvantages with census data. In addition to those problems mentioned in Section 6.1.1, there are special problems in identifying and interviewing residents of long-term care facilities. Census data also have the disadvantage that they are cross-sectional. Information about what happens to a particular group of elderly persons over a period of time, that is longitudinal data, cannot be obtained since the appropriate record linkage is currently not practicable.

Consequently, one usually has to rely on special surveys of individuals, or of programs, to answer specific questions about institutionalization of the elderly. Ideally, a longitudinal survey allows a particular population group, such as the elderly, to be followed to observe the impact of changes as they occur. Although longitudinal studies have considerable advantages, there are difficulties associated with them. Such studies represent a major undertaking and require resources which often are not available. Individuals may be removed from the population because of death or for other reasons. Also, so-called situational effects are likely to arise if subjects and interviewers meet each other frequently. Such frequent meetings may help in maintaining good response rates, but may lead to bias in responding to questions. Moreover, questions may be modified in the course of the study as additional knowledge becomes available, and hence the altered question may be answered in a slightly different manner. Lastly, questions which were not included initially may be incorporated at a later stage.

The following points should be remembered when considering the results of studies which are based on surveys of the institutionalized elderly. If possible, a survey should be based on a representative sample, randomly selected from the population under investigation. It is also important to achieve good response rates since individuals who participate in a survey may differ from those who choose not to participate or who are unavailable to participate. Both of these requirements are difficult to fulfil when dealing with elderly long-term care residents. Moreover, obtaining information from the resident, a relative or the staff may, in each case, involve problems, particularly in ensuring response accuracy. It should be noted that information about associations is sought during the analysis of data obtained from a survey; for example, is institutionalization, or some disease entity which leads to institutionalization, associated with socioeconomic status? If the sample is not a randomly selected sample, it may still be possible to obtain information about the particular association of interest, even though it is difficult to obtain estimates of percentages (for example, on the prevalence of a particular disease) for the population from which the sample was chosen. The establishment of an association represents one step towards the ultimate goal, which is usually the identification of a cause-and-effect relationship. An additional point is that the strength of an association should be estimated and that some estimate of error is provided with any result. Finally, attempts should be made, if possible, to obtain independent verification of the results on subsamples.

These considerations concerning surveys are relevant to a variety of studies involving long-term institutional care, such as how the perception of the quality of care differs depending on the period of time, and the perspective of the individual or the institution; or, an investigation of drug use in an institutionalized population and the short- and long-term effects of such drugs. Hence, studies which are based on surveys should indicate whether the appropriate necessary conditions have been fulfilled or, whether there is at least an awareness of possible shortcomings.

6.1.3 Evaluations

Evaluations of programs and treatment procedures are needed to provide estimates of their effectiveness. Such evaluations are crucial for policy planning and thus eventually for the benefit of clients. They are also aimed, at least in part, at providing information about ways of achieving cost reductions without lowering the quality of care, and this is becoming increasingly important as health-care costs escalate. The evaluation of programs there-fore requires an examination of possible methods for assessing costs and relevant benefits, such as reduced morbidity and mortality. It is also necessary to determine whether the results will apply generally, or only to the population under investigation.

Generally a better answer is obtained from any evaluation if the program is compared with an alternative. A question such as, "Is a new assessment program valuable?" is more meaningful if this particular program is com-pared with some other program, usually the one presently in place. Ques-tions which fail to specify alternatives for comparison are less satisfactory, although questions such as, "How much does it cost to run this assessment program?" can provide important information. To make a comparison meaningful, it is also important to provide a comprehensive description of the various alternatives so that the results can be judged with respect to their relevance in different settings.

There are different aspects of an evaluation. One question is whether a service or program, such as a yearly comprehensive medical check-up of the elderly, is effective with respect to some specific end points. However, the cost of bringing about those desired outcomes must be considered also. In practice both of these aspects of an evaluation may be carried out simultaneously. If the aim is to identify the costs of a program, all relevant costs and consequences for each option should be identified. These costs should include the time and supplies of professional personnel, overhead costs such as capital costs, rent, the costs of light and heat, and the costs which are borne by patients and their relatives or other caregivers. These include actual expenses incurred, as well as the cost of resources which are contributed. For example, families of elderly patients may lose time from work, and volunteers may contribute their time. In addition, there are "hid-den costs" which are frequently borne by patients and their families, such as anxiety and pain. Quantitative estimation of these costs involves assigning numbers to the value and quality of life. Unfortunately, no universally accepted methods are available for doing so (Avorn 1984).

It should be stressed that in a "cost-benefit" analysis, very different results may be obtained depending on whether the viewpoint is that of an institution which organizes the program, that of a patient, the family, or the viewpoint of society. A program may be desirable and cost-effective from the viewpoint of the patient or society but not from the perspective of the institution which would have to provide additional services or modify its procedures.

It is also useful to know how a different methodology could have affected the results. These sensitivity analyses are an important part of a good evaluation. This usually involves repeating the analysis, using different assumptions. If altering the assumptions or estimates used in the analysis does not alter the results significantly, more confidence can be placed in the original results. Conversely, if significant alterations occur in the results, efforts should be made to reduce the uncertainty or to improve the accuracy of the critical assumptions. In reality, it may be useful to give a range of results, and it is also important to be explicit about the various assumptions which have been made in carrying out an evaluation. Thus, a good study should make the reader aware of the various judgements made to arrive at the results, of the viewpoints of the analysis, and of the various caveats which have been used.

Since a thorough evaluation is costly, economic evaluation techniques are most useful when important program objectives require clarification, when the competing alternatives differ significantly, and when large resource commitments are being considered. This, of course, is true for many evaluations involving the institutionalization of the elderly.[2]

6.2 ATTITUDES TOWARDS INSTITUTIONALIZATION

Institutional care of the elderly evokes mixed feelings both in individuals and society generally. Although society is made up of individuals, the perceived relevance of particular events can be very different for individuals, their families and society in general. An obvious example of this is premature death which is of paramount importance to the individual, of some importance to the individual's family, depending on the relationships within the family, and of considerably less importance to society as a whole. In the same way, the attitudes towards institutional care may differ. Attitudes towards old age and the elderly affect both the view of institutional care and the climate within long-term care facilities. Much has been written about society's negative view of older people and the way in which the values of western and urbanized, industrial countries devalue the place of the elderly in the social structure. The syndromes of ageism and gerontophobia are said to be prevalent across Canada (Ontario Council of Health 1978, 84; Schwenger 1985). Not surprisingly, these attitudes influence both those delivering health and social services to the elderly, and those receiving them.

The health and social care professions have been biased towards "the young and potentially employable as the legitimate recipients of service" (Beattie 1976, 627). Not infrequently physicians are reported to be disinterested in and discouraging towards their elderly patients. Schwenger (1985), for example, believes that there is an underemphasis on the potential for rehabilitation among the elderly. There is still a tendency among some health professionals to regard the elderly as a homogeneous group and to stereotype them as either inadequate or incompetent, with the result that health-care workers tend to do things for rather than with the elderly. Kent (1965) quoted Irving Rosow as saying that the problems of old age are those which the elderly actually have and those which experts think they have. A lack of knowledge and interest in institutional care, and the alternatives, means that elderly individuals may not receive the most appropriate care.

These attitudes arise from the emphasis placed on cure and on acute care during the training of physicians and other health professionals. As a result, long-term care of older people has been shaped into a medical, rather than a social, health model (Brody 1977b, 89; Shore 1977, 122). This medical model may be inappropriate for the complete needs of the elderly (see also Section 6.3). However, there is increasing recognition of the relationship between social and health problems, and of the need for co-ordination between institutional and community long-term care. In the education of health professions, more emphasis is being placed on the development of a positive and realistic image of the elderly (see Section 6.4). Research has suggested that more positive attitudes towards the elderly are shown by those professionals who are younger and have had more education (Thorson et al. 1974).

Despite these signs of change, the organization of health resources still tends to be mismatched with the patterns of need found among older adults, and ageism still affects the priorities attached to the distribution of resources. Moreover, the conflict and lack of co-ordination between various levels of government, between government departments and the health professions, and between factions within the health professions, tend to lead to a fragmented service which fails to provide direction or to promote enthusiasm and commitment.

The elderly themselves have strong feelings about giving up their homes and entering long-term institutional care. The majority of elderly people wish to remain in their homes and familiar surroundings. They wish to remain independent and tend to equate institutional living with being dependent. The elderly do not seek over-nurturing environments unless adequate options are unavailable. Indeed, admission to a long-term care facility is too often regarded as the end of the road, a place to await death, rather than as a place which can provide enriching and stimulating experiences, as well as support.

As is mentioned in Section 6.9, an elderly person's admission to institutional care may be unnecessarily influenced by financial steering effects, since it may be less costly for the family to arrange admission than to support their elderly relative at home. However, it has been shown repeatedly that families in general do not neglect or repudiate responsibility for the elderly (Aronson 1985; Brody 1981; Shanas 1979). More often, smaller families, smaller homes, working women and geographical separation of families are responsible for the inability to provide personal care. Indeed, because of the negative view of institutional life, there is often a feeling of guilt on the part of family members. To assist them with the decision to institutionalize a relative, support groups have been set up, which also help with the subsequent adjustment of family and the elderly person (see Section 4.3).

Negative attitudes towards institutional care obscure the fact that for some it may be the most suitable choice. The emphasis on avoiding institutionalization and keeping the frail and sick at home assumes the availability of adequate and appropriate community support services. A supportive family unit is usually necessary as well. Not only may some or all of these requirements be lacking, but also the extent of their effectiveness and the cost in comparison to institutionalization has been questioned (see Section 4.4). Recognition that some decline in late life is inevitable should alter the notion that dependency per se is "bad" and independence "good." It has also been pointed out that to view childhood and old age as dependent phases of life and the years between as independent is too narrow, since in our modern society we are all interdependent (Beattie 1976, 629). Society should understand that a policy choice between either institutional care or community care is not necessary or appropriate. The most important attitude, as Brocklehurst (1977, 235) has said, is that "old people matter." Unfortunately, change in public and professional attitudes does not happen quickly.

6.3 INSTITUTIONALIZATION AND QUALITY OF LIFE

Despite the many good institutions which now exist, concern has been expressed about the quality of life experienced by elderly residents of long-term care facilities. Various studies have shown the effects of environment on behaviour (e.g., Carp 1980; Lawton et al. 1980), including the effect of institutional life on the elderly individual. Too often, it is believed, institutional life is purposeless and the residents powerless, since the predominating model for long-term care facilities remains that of custodial care. In such institutions activities tend to be rigidly structured. Individuality is suppressed as part of a policy of maintaining the facility's rules, and those who conform are regarded as the "better" patients. Residents tend to lack privacy, to have few rights, to be isolated from the outside world and to have little opportunity for stimulating or varied activities. The way in which the building is decorated and furnished emphasizes a standard, utilitarian approach, while residents' personal belongings are restricted to a minimum (Denham 1983, 12–16). The authoritarian attitudes of staff discourage complaints and maintain a social distance between residents and staff. This "closed" system of care tends to have rigid lines of communication with little exchange or development of ideas (Kramer and Kramer 1976, 31). Moreover, the general environment and attitudes make these institutions unattractive, unrewarding and stressful places in which to work, leading to low initiative and morale, and high staff turnover.

Custodial care provides for the physical needs and safety of the residents but ignores their social and psychological needs (Coons 1983, 137). This structured system may be needed in some acute-care settings, but it is not appropriate for elderly persons needing long-term residential care as it fosters the role of the sick, dependent patient. Individuals tend to conform to the expectations of others and, if the only available role is that of the sick patient, residents are likely to adopt the appropriate behaviour. Residents learn in such an environment that the focus is on sickness and disability, and that most care and attention is given to those who are ill, frail and unable to help themselves (Posner 1980). The resident becomes a passive recipient of the care provided, with little encouragement for self-care and no involvement in decisions made about his or her care. This lack of stimulation and responsibility eventually leads to a state of dependency which may be hard to change.

It should be emphasized that though such custodial "bureaucratic" institutions exist, these do not represent all long-term care institutions for the elderly. Moreover, although the negative aspects of this type of institution are generally accepted, there is still discussion about the mechanism and extent of the effects on institutional residents, and the implications for policy and action. Questions which have been raised include (Booth 1985, 2):

(a) Are the deleterious effects of residential care a contingent or an inevitable feature of institutional life?
(b) Do some types of institutional regime have more damaging effects than others?
(c) Do institutional environments affect different residents in different ways?

Even the notion of dependency has a variety of meanings which must be identified before it can be studied. It has been suggested also that, for some individuals, the social, economic and medical benefits of institutionalization may make them feel less disabled, less isolated and more satisfied with life (Myles 1980, 257). This view suggests that the provision of relief through institutional care has a positive effect on residents' identity and morale. Penning and Chappell (1980, 276), on the other hand, have pointed out that perceptions of well-being among elderly institutional residents depend on many factors, including perceived health, perceived economic well-being, autonomy in choosing the residence, informal social relationships and nationality. Their work suggests that neither bureaucratic factors within institutions nor the provision of relief solely explains the effects of institutionalization.

Finding answers to these questions is complicated by a number of conceptual and technical problems such as the extent of institutional variety, differences in the characteristics of residents, and biases in the system of admission to long-term care facilities (Booth 1985, 3–4). Effects attributed to living in an institution may be associated with the anticipation of admission or to the disruption of the admission process. Although loss of independence may be a key factor in relocation stress (see, for example, Grant 1985a), others have suggested that it can be managed when preparation, support and follow-up are available (Borup 1981; Brody et al. 1974; Greenfield 1984; Kasl 1972; Mirotznik and Ruskin 1984; Pablo 1977b). This may be particularly important for those who have experienced a stressful life event prior to admission, such as a sudden deterioration of health or the death of a spouse, and who are more likely to respond negatively with behavioural problems. Another problem may be the range of health and abilities among the residents, from alert to confused and healthy to frail. Within limits, Lawton has suggested, this variability can be enriching, but outside an "optimal range" there may be low morale and resignation (Coons 1983, 139; see also Booth 1985, 219).

Although most if not all residents of long-term care facilities need medical and personal care, this represents only one aspect of their lives. For the residents, the facility is their home and should provide for psychosocial as well as physical and medical needs. The medical treatment, rather than being an end in itself, should be the means by which the individual is able to maintain a varied and satisfying life. The alternative to the custodial, illness-oriented environment, is one which "emphasizes the well aspects of the individual, a point of view which describes the older person in terms of capacities and potential rather than diagnoses and problem behavior" (Coons 1983, 138). Such an environment emphasizes the total person and encourages individuality. By providing roles other than that of the sick patient, such as friend, worker, or consumer, the staff demonstrate expectations which foster well-being and independence. The aim is to provide a quality of life which enables the physically and mentally frail to maintain their dignity, to have the right to make decisions about issues which affect them, and to maintain contact with their past life.

Attempts to lessen the adverse effects of institutionalization in long-term care facilities often depend for their success or failure upon staff attitudes and enthusiasm, but may be expensive in time, money, facilities and resources. It therefore may be necessary to show that a new program is effective by demonstrating measurable improvements in a resident's functioning and quality of life, or, as mentioned previously (Section 5.5.1), by preventing a deterioration which might otherwise have been expected. A variety of scales and tests have been devised to measure the effects of institutionalization on the resident, and the quality of life (see for example, Borup 1981; Denham 1983, 15–16, 22–33; Kane and Kane 1981). The latter include measures of physical and mental health, life satisfaction, morale and quality of the environment.

The institutional environment is influenced by physical factors as well as by the personality and attitudes of staff and residents. It has been stated that the paternalistic and authoritarian attitude of society has "resulted in facilities that are inappropriate in scale, often isolated socially and planned with economies of construction and management as predominant criteria" (Canada Mortgage and Housing Corporation 1979, 2). Attempts are now being made to create a physical environment, as well as a psychological atmosphere, which enhance the image of the elderly person as an individual and help to overcome the erosion of self-respect caused by the drastic change in life-style, including the potential loss of social roles, lack of privacy, regimentation and social isolation. More attention is being paid to the design of long-term care facilities, including site, size and internal features which can provide privacy yet enhance communication between residents and staff. Facilities which provide the opportunity for recreational and social activities, as well as interaction with the community, are believed to encourage an active role and reduce the numbing effects of institutionalization. Moreover, a colourful, well-lit and stimulating environment can provide the cues needed by those adapting to the sensory losses of old age.

For those considering their own or a relative's admission to a long-term care facility, there are many questions which may be asked to identify the nature and philosophy of the facility. Questions such as :

(a) Can residents entertain family, friends, priests, lawyers and others in private and at any time?
(b) Is there an effective residents' committee?
(c) Do staff take time to listen and understand residents' questions and comments?
(d) Are holidays and exchange visits organized by and for the residents? (Cullen 1983, 69; Elliot 1975).

The way in which institutional environments affect elderly residents may vary, but there can be no question that the elderly in need of care, regardless of their illness, can benefit from a broadly based therapeutic program.

6.4 STAFF DEVELOPMENT

The care which residents of long-term institutions receive is dependent, in large measure, on the knowledge and attitudes of the staff. However, until recently professionals working with the elderly received little formal education on the topics of aging and the elderly. In 1978 it was noted that most members of the health and social service professions were exposed in their basic education programs to little more than "a few simple truths concerning the needs of elderly persons" (Ontario Council of Health 1978, 90). Changes have been occurring, however, with professional bodies recognizing the need to incorporate the subject in their curricula (see, for example, Schwab 1983, 565), and many courses and educational programs in gerontology are being developed in universities and community colleges. In some areas nursing homes are being involved actively in professional teaching programs (Aronson 1984; Schneider et al. 1985; Wieland et al. 1986). In addition, there is a need for in-service training or continuing education for professionals already working in the field, and it is this aspect of education which will be considered here.

Recently graduated professionals will have benefitted from the increased attention given to courses on aging and the elderly, but most staff were trained before these opportunities were available. There is a growing recognition of the need for continuing education and there are various ways in which this may be provided. Some institutions are large enough to support their own staff development or in-service program. Others may organize regular or occasional sessions in their facility using faculty from a local community college, university, or other institution. Topics presented are likely to vary depending on the knowledge of the staff and the type of residents in the facility. In addition to skills appropriate to each discipline, the program might include some basic knowledge about the effects of normal aging; common health problems of the elderly and the effects of disability; psychological concerns such as loneliness, depression and abusive behaviour; and some sociological facts such as the position of the elderly in society. The staff should also receive instruction on communication with the patient and family, how to assess a patient, drug side effects, and the value of rehabilitation.[3]

One problem with in-service programs is that staff may complain, often justifiably, that they do not have enough time to attend (see also below). However, changing staff attitudes is as important as providing technical skills and information on the health and psychosocial needs of the elderly. The skill and knowledge which professionals bring to their work with the elderly should be accompanied by patience, kindness and respect. Without these, the residents are likely to remain withdrawn and dependent, and the facility will move little beyond the more traditional custodial care (see Section 6.3). Greater knowledge of the elderly, their role in society, their strengths and disabilities, will promote understanding.

Increased knowledge and changing attitudes will not be successful unless the philosophy and plans of the in-service program are accepted and encouraged by the administration. Efforts to provide more than custodial care, accompanied by staff shortages due to economic constraints, frequently result in severe pressures on the staff. Adequate time, flexible schedules and financial support are all necessary for successful staff development. Moreover there should be recognition, through promotion or salary, of staff members' efforts to increase their knowledge. It should be emphasized that the in-service program should be provided for all staff members, including dietary, housekeeping, maintenance and administrative departments. The chronic nature and multiplicity of problems experienced by the elderly make a multidisciplinary approach to care and treatment essential. Since the intent of staff development is not only to provide knowledge but also to develop understanding of the residents and to promote knowledgeable collaboration between staff, most of the subjects mentioned above are appropriate for all staff.

Another reason to encourage staff development in long-term care institutions is to boost morale. Work with long-stay, elderly people can be difficult and stressful, often leading to "burn-out." European countries, faced with large increases in the elderly members of the population, are concerned about being able to attract enough staff for long-term care (Nusberg 1984, 80). In efforts to upgrade these careers there is increasing emphasis on professional training and continuing education. An improved and more professional image through greater knowledge and skill, and more multidisciplinary involvement in decisions regarding care, will lead to increased enthusiasm, a sense of purpose, and commitment.

6.5 EXCESSIVE MEDICATION[4]

The elderly are more at risk than other age groups of developing adverse drug reactions which may require hospital admission and may even be fatal. It is not known to what extent these are a reflection of improper use and to what extent inherently imperfect drugs are responsible. It is widely believed that prescribing for the elderly is often done poorly (see, for example, Shaw 1982). Specifically, over-medication of the elderly, and the medicolegal implications of involuntary restrictions of an individual's liberty by the use of psychotropic drugs (Schafer 1985) are subjects of increasing concern. Schmidt et al. (1977) report that mentally ill patients in nursing homes showed a gradual increase in prescribed psychoactive medication and a decrease in activity. They suggest that the consequences of this raise serious questions about the care of the psychiatric patient. It is also recognized that inaccurate diagnosis results in misuse of psychotropic medication (Salzman 1981), and this is of particular importance among the elderly.

It has been stressed that professional drug surveillance is crucial for improving the therapeutic process. It has been recommended, for example, that records should be kept of the conditions under which a prescribed drug is administered, and that a strong effort should be made to reduce the number of drugs prescribed (Ingman et al. 1975). However, considerable reorganization will be necessary in most extended care facilities to achieve such changes. Apart from these more medical aspects, other factors, such as staff-patient ratios and the quality of staff employed, affect drug usage. The problem of excessive medication provides an excellent example of the need for a multidisciplinary approach to a problem which is of major importance to the elderly.

Metabolism of drugs is affected, although in different ways, by the age of elderly individuals. These age-associated changes have been documented and include decreases in renal function, cardiac output, lean body mass, total body water, serum albumin concentration and drug metabolizing enzyme activity (Crooks et al. 1976; Gorrod 1974; Sellers 1985; Triggs et al. 1975). Moreover, studies have shown that adverse drug reactions increase with age (Greenblatt et al. 1977; Miller 1973). Drug reactions have been reported in 10 to 25% of admissions to geriatric hospitals, and in one study adverse reactions were judged to be the sole cause of at least 16% of admis-

sions to a psychogeriatric unit (Shaw 1982). Moreover, interactions are frequent (Hussar 1985; Prien et al. 1976); a recent study reports that nearly
24% of elderly patients admitted to general and geriatric units of a teaching
hospital were receiving drugs with known interacting effects (Gosney and
Tallis 1984).

The increased susceptibility of elderly patients to adverse drug reaction is
ascribed, at least in part, to age-related pharmacological changes that result
in different amounts of drug reaching the site of action, compared with
younger patients. Little is known about how drugs interact with each other
and with other factors, such as the nutritional status of the elderly, or the
presence of disease (Bowman and Rosenberg 1982).

Many conditions of the elderly do not require drug treatment. There is
doubt, for example, whether drug treatment of mild hypertension is appropriate (see also Guttmacher et al. 1981; Kuramoto and Matsushita 1985;
The Lancet 1985a). Even the blood pressure values which define the degree
of hypertension vary by country, and may change over time. The benefits
of treatment compared with the risks should be considered, and unnecessarily prolonged drug therapy should be avoided.

There is thus a need for research on drug interaction and the adverse
effects of drugs. Such studies should include the interaction of drugs with
diet and social and medical conditions, and could follow a relatively large
number of elderly individuals longitudinally. There is also the general question of how to determine rational and cost-effective drug therapy (Tribble
1985). Studies should investigate which prescribing, dispensing and
monitoring systems are practical and effective in helping the elderly and
their prescribers to use drugs more effectively. A report of the Phar-
maceutical Manufacturers Association believes that drugs are cost-effective
(Brink 1985), but one might suspect bias. This is certainly a major issue
involving a number of questions (see Section 6.1.3). Specific actions which
have been proposed include simplifying the drug regimen prescribed by the
physician. That is, to reduce the regimen to the fewest drugs, the smallest
number of pills, and the longest dose intervals practical. Questions which
should be asked are whether medicine taken four times daily can be given
twice a day at a higher dosage or even at the same dosage, whether a single
drug can suffice for two, and whether medications can be given at the same
time. It is also desirable to plan the drug schedule around the patient's
schedule and not vice-versa, so that it does not intrude but blends in with
the rest of life (Kroenke 1985).

6.6 INAPPROPRIATE PLACEMENT

Canada, like many other countries, is faced with considerable growth in the
proportion of the elderly in the population (see Chapter 3). It is also known
that increased age leads to greater use of health- care services. At the same
time, Roos et al. (1984) noted that only a relatively small proportion of the

elderly account for the majority of hospital days used by the elderly. They suggest that health-care utilization patterns are determined primarily by health-care professionals rather than by the characteristics of elderly patients. However, there is little question that inappropriate placement and use of facilities occur (see also Section 4.2). As Fisher and Zorzitto (1983) have noted:

> ... emergency departments are often used inappropriately, particularly at night and on weekends, to gain access to the health care system. Pressures on patients and their families inevitably reach a breaking point, since neither community nor medical and social services are well equipped to identify problems at an early stage and respond to them. Moreover, once elderly patients are admitted under such circumstances they are more likely to be inappropriately labelled as placement problems because of the staff's lack of understanding of their potential for improvement.

The arbitrariness of the decision-making process within the health-care system is also suggested by the substantial differences in the mean length of a stay in general hospitals in different countries (Heikkinen et al. 1983). This suggests that the policies prevalent in different locations, and the influence of health care professionals primarily determine the usage of hospital days by the elderly. It seems likely that the availability of hospital space, together with the availability of community services, rather than the degree of need, determine to an appreciable extent whether a frail elderly person will be placed in a hospital.

A similar argument applies to the availability of physicians, since if appropriately qualified physicans become available in increasing numbers, it is probable that they will find employment in caring for the elderly. The number of available physicians, like the number of available beds, is thus likely to be a major factor in determining the usage of institutional facilities.

There is a substantial proportion of the elderly who are cared for at home on a long-term basis by their relatives. It is not known how large this proportion is, but it seems certain that the characteristics of this population of elderly persons differ from those of the elderly receiving long-term care in institutions, and not only with respect to the severity of their disease. Many relatives would only place the elderly person in an institution if they were reasonably sure that he or she would receive as good care in an institution as they are able to provide in their homes. On the other hand, some families may readily place an elderly relative in an institution if a bed is available. The appropriate balance between community care and institutional care is an important question (see Chapter 4). International comparisons show large differences between and within regions (Factor and Habib 1985), as are also found for other medical services. For example, in Israel there are only 0.9 acute-care beds per thousand elderly (compared with an English guideline of 2.2 beds per thousand), but there are 8.2 nursing care beds per thousand elderly (compared with the guideline of 3.7 per thousand in England) (Ginsberg 1985).

Most available data suggest that Canada institutionalizes more of the elderly than some other developed countries, specifically the United States, and England and Wales (see Section 3.3). This high rate is probably not because of a relatively greater need for institutional care in Canada. In fact, it has been shown that many residents of long-term care facilities could be cared for more appropriately in alternative settings (Kraus et al. 1976b). Women, particularly, may be institutionalized unnecessarily (Dulude 1978, 82–94). A widely held belief is that institutional care should be prevented or avoided whenever possible, since the restrictive environments of such settings tend not to be health-enhancing (see Chapter 4).[5] There is a growing awareness of the problem of inappropriate placement and a variety of systems have been set up to overcome this problem (see Section 4.2). However, evaluations of different types of placement co-ordination service are needed. For example, one question to ask is whether the service should be responsible for assessing clients; this would affect the number and type of staff needed by the placement service.

In order to place an individual at the level of care which is most beneficial for his or her needs, it has been suggested that a multidisciplinary assessment tool should be employed as is done, for example, in the home-care programs of British Columbia and Manitoba. Such an assessment tool should address the relevant needs and the available options for matching these needs. A standardized assessment also facilitates the implementation of the appropriate measures if an individual has to be moved from one part of the health-care system to another. As noted earlier (Section 6.1.3), there are indications that assessments of perceived needs will vary depending on who is making the judgement (see, for example, Kaban and Block 1984). Also, assessments should be updated at regular intervals, in order to detect changes in the individual's needs (see Dobrof et al. 1980).

The success of any procedure to reduce inappropriate placement will be influenced by the involvement of family members in the decision-making process (Dobrof et al. 1980). This, however, may raise difficulties since the interests of the elderly person and of family members may not be identical. For example, the individual may prefer to remain in his or her home whereas family members may believe that the individual has unrealistic ideas of what he or she can manage to do, and be unable to provide assistance. This may also lead to conflicts which have legal and financial implications.

6.7 FUNDING AND STAFFING PROBLEMS

In attempting to improve the health-care system, including institutional care, it is tempting to plead for additional funding. However, with the present economic climate this is perhaps unrealistic. It may be more appropriate to consider that the funds available for the needs of the elderly will remain approximately constant in spite of the increasing proportion of the elderly, particularly those eighty-five and over. In support of this statement there are indications that the funding of the Canadian health-care system is comparable, as a proportion of GDP, to funding in other countries (see Table 6.1). If this is the case, the task is to re-examine priorities in the social and health-care services and, on the basis of such studies, to reallocate funds more appropriately.

Questions arise concerning the criteria for institutionalization, how many beds should be made available in old people's homes, nursing homes, and chronic care hospitals, and how much should be allocated to home support services, day care centres and day hospitals. This is a difficult task and it is unfortunate that few evaluations have been carried out of programs presently in place. It is impossible therefore at this stage to arrive at appropriate proportions. However, one can draw attention to some of the difficulties which might be overcome by more careful evaluations. Some of these areas of concern are discussed next.

6.7.1 Estimating the Number of Required Beds

In planning for the health care needs of the frail elderly, questions arise concerning the number of beds needed. There is no simple answer since this "need" will depend not only on the nature of the medical and social problems of the population, but also on the preferences of the elderly and their families. If families are prepared and able to undertake a continuing and even greater burden of care, the need for institutionalization may be

TABLE 6.1

HEALTH CARE EXPENDITURES AS A PROPORTION OF
GROSS DOMESTIC PRODUCT (GDP), 1960–1983

	Percentage of Total Expenditure on Health in GDP		
	1960	1975	1983
Australia	5.1	7.6	7.5
Austria	4.4	6.4	7.3
Canada	5.5	7.4	8.5
Finland	4.2	5.8	6.6
France	4.3	7.6	9.3
Germany	4.8	8.1	8.2
Greece	2.9	4.0	4.7
Italy	3.9	6.7	7.4
Japan	3.0	5.7	6.7
Netherlands	3.9	7.7	8.8
Sweden	4.7	8.0	9.6
United Kingdom	3.9	5.5	6.2
United States	5.3	8.6	10.8

SOURCE: Iglehart, 1986, p. 205. Reprinted by permission of the *New England Journal of Medicine*.

reduced, although this may entail considerable stress for the family providing the care (Cantor 1983).

One approach which has been used to estimate the number of required beds, is a waiting-list survey, in which an estimate is made of the number of people waiting for a bed in a long-term care facility. However, such surveys may include those who are on more than one institution's waiting list and may not take into account those people currently occupying beds, who would not need to do so if appropriate home care and other services were available. Further, it is undesirable to provide sufficient beds to abolish waiting lists, since institution administrators then might be tempted to fill empty beds, which generally are not funded, with patients who could be situated more appropriately elsewhere.

Since there are difficulties with waiting-list surveys, one cannot be confident that there is a serious deficiency of beds. Such surveys can be a method of estimating the need for institutional beds, but they should be used with care. In addition, waiting times should be considered. A long waiting list may include names entered for more than one facility or doubtful cases of need. Such individuals may not take an offered place, and waiting time for others on the list is therefore relatively short. A lengthy waiting time suggests that the list contains genuine applications.

An alternative is that a certain percentage of beds are made available on the basis of the experience in other jurisdictions. A figure of fifty extended care beds (in long-term care wards or institutions) per thousand over-sixty-five population, has been suggested, but it is known that there are large variations in bed usage, even within one country (Factor and Habib 1985). Moreover, it is likely that a lower figure would be sufficient if, and perhaps only if, more community support services were available. For example in Japan, where cohabitation with an adult child is still the rule, the provision of long-term care beds is as low as about fifteen per thousand (Nusberg 1984, 71). Another proposed method is to estimate the number of beds required on the basis of functional status in a representative sample (Ginsberg 1985). Ginsberg recommends an approach which involves the definition of the relevant packages of care, the measurement of dysfunction among the elderly, and a costing of the various care packages.

It should be noted that additional beds may be an embarrassment rather than an asset if the necessary supporting services, and particularly the necessary number of nurses and rehabilitation staff, are not available (Collings 1985). Moreover, this might lead to inadequate funding for non-institutional services, even if they can be shown to provide for the needs of the elderly in a better and more cost-effective manner.

6.7.2 The Optimal Size of an Institution and of Individual Nursing Units

Determining the optimal size of a hospital, nursing or residential-care home must take into consideration the provision of an acceptable quality of care at a reasonable cost. Although costs are not the only issue, there may be some economies if such institutions become larger. On the other hand, a point may be reached when costs per client increase markedly because of the administrative difficulty of managing a relatively large facility.

The optimal size of institutions caring for the elderly has not been studied thoroughly, but aspects of this question have been investigated. For example, Mor et al. (1985) have found that small residential-care homes (one to six beds) spend considerably more on food per person than homes with over twenty-one beds, suggesting substantial economies of scale. For hospitals ranging in size from under one hundred to over four hundred beds, the total operating costs per bed generally increased with size (Bentkover et al. 1984, 217). However, the initial capital costs per bed may be relatively greater for smaller institutions. Larger, more institutional homes had higher staffing costs per client than smaller homes, presumably because the caretaking time of the owners of small homes was not taken into account. There are also a number of confounding variables, such as the type of residents served. For example, small home owners may be more willing to exert the extra effort required by a physically ill resident than that required by residents with a psychiatric history. In fact, owner-occupied homes have been reported to be less likely to house former mental patients. Another variable in establishing costs will be the amount of nursing care required and/or provided.

The Ontario Ministry of Health's guidelines (1977) suggest that an ideal chronic care unit should contain 36 ± 4 beds or multiples thereof. However, as noted earlier, economic considerations are not the only ones, since attention should also be paid to psychosocial issues. Riportella-Muller and Slesinger (1982), for example, found a positive correlation between unit size and complaints about administrative procedures, services rendered and the physical plant. Greenwald and Linn (1971) noted that patient satisfaction and activity levels declined as nursing unit size increased. Curry and Ratliff (1973) reported that more than 20% of the patients in larger nursing homes were isolated from their friends and family compared with 5% in smaller nursing homes. Ullmann (1981) has argued that a small unit size is conducive to a greater degree of staff-patient contact, which may increase the accuracy of assessments of patient needs and may lead to more appropriate therapeutic programs. Moos suggested that an increased unit size decreases patient independence and staff involvement, leads to fewer spontaneous relationships between staff and patients, a decreased emphasis on understanding patients' problems, an increased rigidity in the structure of the unit and an increased need by staff to control and manage patients. In a study of wards in a Veterans Administration hospital, Moos (1974, 130–31; 198) reported that successful small wards were characterized by a greater emphasis on personal responsibility, leading to a supportive and helpful environment, whereas successful large wards emphasized staff control and an ordered environment with little focus on patient autonomy. Kayser-

Jones (1986) suggests that for some residents with multiple functional disabilities an open ward represents a more supportive environment.

Another consideration affecting the size of an institution is that there may be an advantage if chronic care facilities, nursing homes and old people's homes, retirement villages (or other forms of sheltered housing), and day-care centres are placed in adjoining locations so that each elderly person would have ready access to another level of care without having to move very far. A disadvantage is that such complexes will need considerable space that may not be available in the areas close to community facilities. Such proximity is desirable, since it facilitates the integration of long-term care residents with the general community.

6.8 DIVIDED JURISDICTIONAL RESPONSIBILITY

One of the problems faced by administrators who attempt to provide a continuum of care is that the responsibility for the well-being of the elderly may not rest with one government department. This creates confusion for the individual residents, their families, and for the institution if it attempts to provide a comprehensive range of services. The provinces deal with this in different ways, but some of the relevant responsibilities rest with departments of health, whereas other responsibilities are with provincial departments of community and social services or related ministries. There has been an awareness of this problem for some time and discussions have taken place, but no generally accepted solution has been reached.

The question is important since, depending on who has the main responsibility for providing the funds for the components of care, different funding patterns may prevail and these funding patterns will determine how the continuum of care is provided. A ministry of health and social services would appear to have much to recommend it. However Manitoba, where such a system was in place, has abandoned the concept although in practice maintaining close co-operation at the local level (personal communications from Dr. N. Chappell 1986 and Miss B. Havens 1987). Such a ministry may be too large to function as a well-integrated organization, since the temptation would be to divide it into two parts, one dealing with health, and the other with social services.

The development of linkages between the health and social services responsible for the elderly is important at all levels, including the local level. For example, in Ontario there are district health councils which make recommendations to the provincial department of health. In theory, this can be regarded as desirable since it is local people who should be involved in the planning process, as occurs in a number of other countries. Social planning councils, and similar organizations, have also been established to make recommendations for the community care of the elderly. Whatever the appropriate administrative structure, a continuum of care for the frail elderly should include physical, psychosocial and economic considerations, which together embody the holistic view of "health" emphasized by the World Health Organization (1978). Possibly, local organizations could be set up which would deal specifically with the needs of the elderly and which might report to appropriate provincial ministries. However, since programs involving the elderly are interrelated, there may be problems in obtaining funding if this involves transfer of funds from one budget to another. Nor is it clear who will have the responsibility for resolving the conflicting claims for funds which may arise in this way. Local examples of "health complexes" have been reported which co-ordinate their activities, although the different units of the complex have separate boards responsible to different provincial ministries (Draper 1985).

6.9 ECONOMIC STEERING EFFECTS

As mentioned earlier (Section 2.8), in some provinces such as Ontario, there are financial steering effects which may affect the rates of institutionalization. Specifically, residential care leads to a greater financial burden for the patient than extended care, while chronic care in a hospital costs nothing for the first sixty days. Although there is evidence that family members provide considerable informal support for their elderly relatives who live in the community (see Sections 4.1 and 4.4), there may be a tendency, when institutional care is needed, to seek admission to an unnecessarily high level of care either for financial reasons or to forestall a further move if deterioration occurs in the resident's condition.

The role of the family is crucial. The World Health Organization (1984) has said that:

> The family is the greatest single source of support and the centre of activity for most elderly people ... The decrease in the number of children, and their dispersion owing to migration and urbanization, means that care for dependent old parents cannot be easily shared by several siblings. Moreover, family care of an elderly person almost always means in effect care by a daughter or daughter-in-law, and the changing role of women and their participation in the labour force further diminishes the chance of family support.

This provides a good example of an area where economic incentives could be provided to enable a person to remain within the family, as is done in a number of European countries (Gibson 1984, 169–71; see also Aronson 1985). Community service support such as respite care may be helpful (see also Section 4.3), but the costs of caring for a sick person are considerable (see, for example, Berk and Wilensky 1985; Bloom et al. 1985). One way to ease this financial burden is to provide a tax exemption or direct payment to a family looking after an elderly relative who otherwise would have to be placed in an institution. These payments may be designated specifically for institutional or home care. Although each of these methods would have administrative difficulties, they should be explored more widely and perhaps tested in different parts of Canada. However, financial difficulties are not as pervasive an issue as might be expected (Cantor 1983).

Economic steering effects may also be important in the debate over the role of government operated and privately operated institutions. Privately operated facilities may be more efficient (in economic terms) than those that are government operated, but may not provide all the needed services. Although the appropriate evaluations have not been carried out, it is believed that the quality of care is generally higher in the public and non-profit homes than in the for-profit homes (Lemke and Moos 1986; Nusberg 1984, 71; see also Gray 1986; Mor et al. 1986). Whatever the results of such evaluations, the challenge is to provide financial incentives for institutions which are providing good care, since present financing policies have generally not been designed with much consideration of these incentives.

The challenge for administrators of long-term care facilities is that they may have to make do with available funds, while maintaining an acceptable or better standard of care. In other words, if numbers cared for, or profitability, as defined in any way, is viewed as an indicator of efficiency, this is likely to be in conflict with what may be described as the effectiveness, or quality of the programs. The trade-off between these two goals is not easy but it is one that administrators should consider, since actual or perceived resource shortages will sooner or later require some difficult choices. For example, attempts to enhance efficiency, or profitability, through reduced staffing, equipment or supplies will inevitably tend to reduce quality (Fottler et al. 1981). Nonetheless, there are indications that a positive relationship between efficiency and quality of care is possible. For example, Longest (1978) reported that hospitals which organize services in an efficient manner also tend to provide higher quality service than those which operate less efficiently. One way of achieving efficiency and quality of care is to provide the appropriate economic incentives. We, as a society, have not defined the quality of institutional care we want and for which we are willing to pay. Moreover, efforts to "control" institutions have focussed on the process of sevice delivery, rather than on outcomes, and cost-effective innovations are generally not rewarded (Smith and Fottler 1981). Presumably a policy which rewards administrators for attaining defined outcomes, by some measure of both efficiency and quality of care, can provide a stimulus to managerial creativity. An experimental protocol along these lines has been developed in Israel (Wartski and Tulchinsky 1985) involving a scoring schedule which included measures of medical care, nursing care, nutrition, physiotherapy, occupational activities, social support systems and the facility itself.

Such a reward system could be established, but would require the development of a management information system, based on data provided by each institution, on a wide variety of patient care quality indicators. Measures such as functional capacity, social or emotional behaviour, and changes in these measures, could be used, together with the amount of medical and nursing care provided, the availability of services such as physiotherapy and social support systems, and the physical state of the buildings. Reimbursement formulas could then be developed to fund institutions, based on whether they are below average, average or above average in these outcome measures (Fottler et al. 1981; Wartski and Tulchinsky 1985).

Another illustration of the importance of economic steering effects is provided by the question of who should be mainly responsible for the medical care of the institutionalized elderly. Some groups believe that the general practitioner is the most appropriate person to do this, others believe that it should be the geriatrician, others believe that it should be nurse practitioners, and yet others that the team approach is most appropriate (see also Section 7.1). There are numerous other related issues that are susceptible to economic steering, such as should physicians serving the institutionalized elderly be employed on a fee-for-service basis or on salary. Economic measures could also be employed to encourage various forms of self-help, for example, by paying travel expenses to volunteers and by supporting the elderly to help each other.

6.10 SUMMARY AND CONCLUSIONS

The present chapter aims to stress areas where changes should, and are likely, to occur. These changes are identified by considering various sources of concern, that is, areas where there are reasons to believe that the present organization could be improved. In discussing these areas, it is realized that there are no simple remedies.

The areas of concern which are discussed in this chapter are the lack of good data; attitudes towards institutionalization; the quality of life in institutions; the problems arising from excessive medications; inappropriate placement; the general issue of funding and staffing problems, with particular reference to the value of waiting lists and the optimal size of facilities; the problems arising from a divided jurisdictional responsibility; and the neglect of economic steering effects that can be used to achieve desirable goals.

The following may be concluded:

1. Reliable data on the elderly population, particularly on those over age eighty-five, are limited in scope and detail, and it is usually necessary to carry out well-conducted surveys to obtain adequate information. Longitudinal surveys are often desirable but difficult to conduct successfully.

2. Evaluations of existing programs are crucial since many new approaches are being recommended and implemented. It is important to make sure that these programs are effective in attaining their intended aims.

3. Attitudes towards long-term institutional care are changing for the better, but much remains to be done. The general attitude which equates "aging" with "illness" should be altered.

4. The quality of life in institutions could be improved, mainly by changing what is frequently a paternalistic and authoritarian attitude to one which enhances the image of the elderly resident by encouraging independence and personal autonomy.

5. To improve care and prevent unnecessary illness in the elderly, it is important to investigate which prescribing, dispensing and monitoring system can help the elderly and the prescribers use drugs more knowledgeably and effectively.

6. There is little question that inappropriate placement occurs frequently, partly because of a lack of alternatives. Placement coordination and similar services can help to overcome this problem, since it is hard for the frail elderly and for service providers to be aware of the plethora of federal, provincial, municipal and voluntary aging programs. A "best" method of operating such services has not been identified; indeed it is likely that various formats will be successful under different circumstances.

7. Since there are large differences in the proportion of elderly who are institutionalized in different jurisdictions, it seems important to investigate reasons for these differences and to re-examine priorities within the social and health-care services.

8. With respect to funding and staffing problems, it is pointed out that waiting lists should be used with care; waiting time should also be considered.

9. It seems that there are advantages in having relatively small units within an institution. The placement of different types of institutions in adjoining locations to facilitate the transfer of patients should be considered.

10. A divided jurisdictional responsibility, where ministries of health respond to health needs and ministries of social services respond to social needs and poverty, gives rise to problems with the coordination of services. It is believed that it would be desirable to combine social and health-service planning mechanisms, particularly at the local level.

11. Economic steering effects can be important in achieving desired aims, but have not been used as much as they might have been. Moreover, at present some economic steering effects tend to move people to a more intensive level of care. These mechanisms should be used to facilitate desirable developments, such as involving the families of the frail elderly if they wish to help. Methods should be developed to provide financial incentives not only to lessen the dependence on institutional care, but also to improve the quality of institutional care.

NOTES

1. A number of books explain the relevant theory, such as *Statistics* by Freedman, Pisani and Purves (1978).
2. Additional readings on evaluations are available from a host of publications. One relevant book in this area is a publication entitled *Evaluative Research on Social Programs for the Elderly* (O'Brien and Streib 1977) which also contains a number of useful references. A Canadian publication which outlines many of the important points in a precise but comprehensive manner is an article by Stoddart and Drummond (1984) entitled *How to Read Clinical Journals: VII. To Understand an Economic Evaluation (Part B)*, on which many points in this section are based.
3. One way to assess the knowledge of staff, whether before or after the educational program, is to use the "Facts on Aging Quiz" devised by Palmore (1977), which has been validated for Canadian use, with minor modification of demographic questions, by Matthews et al. (1984); but see also Norris et al. 1987.
4. For a fuller discussion of drugs and aging, see McKim and Mishara (1987).
5. In economic terms, Gross and Schwenger (1981, 119) estimate that as much as 100 million dollars would have been saved in 1976 if elderly patients in Ontario had been placed in optimal settings. As another example, Blum and Minkler (1980) estimate that up to 90% of nursing home patients in California could have been cared for appropriately in settings providing less heavy care.

CHAPTER 7

FUTURE DIRECTIONS FOR POLICY AND RESEARCH

This chapter examines possible developments towards improving the quality of institutional care and outlines some research which may ensure that these changes are effective through the development and testing of alternative models of care. As mentioned in Section 6.1.3, such evaluations should include a comparison with at least one alternative. The chapter relies on methodology which has been discussed earlier, and focusses on some of the problems which have been noted in previous chapters. Research is not a panacea for all problems relating to institutional care of the elderly since education and funding, for example, are also important. However, this is an area where research can play a most useful role, and some possible research areas are discussed in the next two sections.

7.1 RESEARCH ON THE QUALITY OF CARE

Concerns have been expressed frequently about the quality of care provided in institutions caring for the elderly, particularly in view of the impending demographic changes (Andrews 1985; McDaniel 1986; Watson et al. 1984). The challenge is to find ways to permit more autonomy, independence, decision making and privacy for residents, and to provide more opportunities to utilize the remaining capabilities of the frail elderly in social activities and in worthwhile roles and tasks. Such research should be able to provide some answers if the questions have been defined clearly. Although, as mentioned in Section 6.1.3, longitudinal studies have a number of difficulties associated with them, and are rarely conducted, they are the type of studies most likely to provide definitive answers concerning quality of care. Some interesting experimental programs are being implemented (see for example Chambers et al. 1983; Schuman et al. 1978, 1980). Geriatric teaching programs, problem-oriented medical records, a philosophy of rehabilitation and a team approach are among the ideas being emphasized.

Specific aspects of quality of care and evaluation of programs which are being investigated include the following:

1. One area identified previously (Section 6.5) is the use of excessive medication by the elderly, who are at risk because of the effects of drug interactions and of drug toxicity. The need to carry out studies in these areas has been recognized widely, and is considered a matter of priority (McKim and Mishara 1987). Studies along these lines, carried out with institutionalized elderly, can also be expected to be of value to non-institutionalized elderly persons.

2. As mentioned in Section 6.9, there has been considerable debate about who is the most appropriate person to be responsible for the care of the institutionalized elderly. No conclusions have been reached about the optimal role of the general practitioner and the specialist in geriatric medicine, nor the benefits of a team approach (Allen et al. 1986; Hoffbrand 1985; Ontario Medical Association 1984; Steel 1985; Williams 1986). In principle a team approach appears attractive, but there remains the question of how effectively a team can collaborate. Individuals who have worked in institutions may support such a system, but it is the role of the epidemiologist to devise appropriate trials to test the effectiveness. One view is that, although the physician is trained in making a diagnosis and prognosis, his or her training is less suited to providing "care." Hence, it may be more appropriate for nurses to have the main responsibility for organizing and integrating the care of the elderly. Leaving cost considerations aside, it could be argued that physicians are best able to co-ordinate the different disciplines involved. Yet, there is growing discussion over the need for a more social, as opposed to a medical, approach to the care of the elderly and of the importance of including other disciplines, such as the social worker. The relative importance of day hospitals, day care and social networks in providing support to the frail elderly living in the community is related to this issue.

3. Another question is whether there should be special facilities for the elderly requiring long-term care, or for certain groups of elderly such as the mentally ill or cognitively impaired, or whether such segregation is unreasonable and unnecessary (Peace 1984, 106). If the patients are integrated in one facility, the mentally ill may be shunned by both staff and other patients. On the other hand, a disadvantage of segregation is that it is less easy to obtain access to the various specialists who may be required. It would be useful to know how different countries approach this question, and to determine which method or methods are best able to balance the needs of the residents and staff within necessary financial constraints.

4. There are also many considerations associated with the care of the dying. For example, should palliative care be provided in special locations, or should this type of care be available within any insti-

tution. The hospice movement has attracted attention and appears to have had considerable success. However, there are still a number of issues, such as costs, patient rights and commitment of physicians, which need to be clarified (Aiken 1986; Bayer et al. 1983; Greer and Mor 1986; Greer et al. 1986; Hadlock 1985).

5. Another area which requires investigation is the extent and quality of various home support and other community care services and how these relate to institutionalization (see Chapter 4). Community health-care services for the elderly involve many professions and it is not clear what combinations of professional and non-professional services are most appropriate. Currently only about 2% of the expenditures for the elderly are in the area of community-based services, while long-term care, health-care and income-support programs represent the major forms of assistance.

   It is believed that a good home-support system will enable more people to remain at home. It might be expected that in countries, or in provinces, where better home-support services are available, less institutionalization is required. However, there is little evidence for this (Kane and Kane 1985b), possibly because the elderly who use such services differ from those who tend to be institutionalized. Certainly, the relationship between institutionalization of the elderly and the number of community-support services is confounded by a number of other factors, such as the total budget available for the care of the elderly, and the quality of services that are available. Cost-effectiveness is an important consideration (Clarfield 1983), including the role of financial support for family care at home.

6. The role of the family is of importance to the elderly. However, specific ways should be investigated in which the family can be involved in looking after the frail or ill elderly most effectively (see, for example, Glosser and Wexler 1985). Courses for family members who are willing and able to look after the frail elderly may be of value (see Section 4.3) and, generally, services which provide support and relief for the caregiver need development.

7. A careful and comprehensive assessment of an individual is more likely to ensure that an appropriate care plan is obtained and that monitoring of progress occurs (Kane and Kane 1981; Kohn 1983; Pfeiffer 1975). Various assessment tools have been designed, but many consider mainly physical health and exclude other aspects of quality of life. The advent of the computer into institutions will facilitate the acquistion and use of such information (Whiting-O'Keefe et al. 1985).

8. In Section 6.7, the absence of data on appropriate staffing patterns and unit sizes was noted. One method of investigating this type of problem is to carry out a clinical trial in which two groups of

patients are randomly assigned to two facilities of different unit sizes or with different staffing patterns. Then differences that become apparent over time should be investigated. In practice, this is not a realistic way of proceeding since the required double-blind procedure (to ensure that only the treatment and no other factor affects the outcome measure) is not feasible. However, by comparing two similar populations which are housed in units of different size, but which are otherwise similar, it should be possible to carry out some evaluations, again in terms of some predetermined outcome measures (see Section 6.1.3). It should also be noted that unit size is not the only factor, since the internal configuration of buildings and other architectural aspects are likely to have a major impact on the desirability of various facilities. These issues represent a challenge for architects, planners and related professionals.

7.2 RESEARCH ON PREVENTIVE MEASURES AND OUTCOMES OF CARE

In the previous section some questions were identified which relate to the quality of care. These questions generally involved outcomes which occurred either immediately or in the reasonably near future. The present section will emphasize preventive measures and thus a greater time span; that is, programs and procedures aimed to prevent or delay illness, and which might be initiated if they can show a marked effect on health status (see also Gray 1985; Nusberg 1984, 76–79). The comments made about the need for appropriate research and the importance of taking into account the costs of the various programs, which have been stressed in Section 6.1.3, again apply to this section.

The need for prevention is obvious. Yet, work on prevention does not always receive the priority which it should (Watson et al. 1984, Chapter 6). If one wishes to reduce the proportion of the elderly who are placed in institutions, programs are needed to detect early signs of disorders which are likely to lead to institutionalization, and/or to identify those elderly who are at greatest risk of requiring institutional care. The following are areas needing investigation:

1. The predictors of institutionalization are numerous and could involve diet, financial considerations, social isolation, stresses which occur within the family, the unsatisfactory nature of some of the features in the individual's home and progressing disability. Each of these may affect the functional ability of the individual. One method of carrying out preventive action could be to involve the family physician, but there are two problems with this; one is that this approach may be expensive, and secondly, the physician may not have the background, inclination or time to investigate in detail the various psychosocial and economic factors which could

lead to institutionalization. Alternatives that should be examined include whether other professionals such as public health nurses, health visitors or social workers could carry out these tasks effectively, on the understanding that if a medical problem is apparent, a physician would be involved. To carry out an evaluation of such a program would involve a longitudinal study, perhaps along the lines of the study by Spitzer et al. (1974), or that by Rubenstein et al. (1984).

2. Action to prevent long-term institutional care may also be possible at an acute care hospital. If an elderly patient is admitted, a useful preventive measure might be to review the possible need for and alternatives to institutionalization before discharge from the acute care facility. It would also be of interest to investigate the factors which determine whether an individual is institutionalized after an event such as a hip fracture.

3. Elderly persons with impaired mental function are at risk of premature institutionalization. Early diagnosis is important. Also important is the question of how the family, the physician and various community care programs can assist the person to remain at home. Related to this is the effectiveness of protective monitoring and housing, and which particular aspects would be most appropriate and cost-effective (see, for example, Gilleard 1985).

4. Another area of prevention concerns various life-style variables such as the absence of safety features in homes, physical inactivity, cigarette smoking, nutrition, etc. Modification of life-style variables which affect life expectancy may be difficult for the elderly since it is often hard to change one's habits in the later years. Such changes in old age may be too late to be effective, but there is little doubt that preventive intervention can be important. Different risks vary in their importance depending on the number of people affected, the magnitude of the resulting changes and the strength of the evidence. For example, the effect of cigarette smoking on mortality is well established even in the elderly (Branch and Jette 1984; Gentleman et al. 1978). There is good evidence that giving up smoking leads to a better life expectancy and better health, in addition to reducing the risk of fire. Similar evidence is not yet available for a number of other risk factors. The case for direct preventive measures such as installing safety features in homes is more immediately obvious, but the quantitative evaluations of the relevant outcomes are less well documented.

7.3 POLICY AND PROGRAM IMPLICATIONS

There are essentially two considerations in planning long-term care; the prevention of institutionalization, and the provision of care for the elderly once they are in institutions. Some of the research issues relating to these questions have been outlined in Sections 7.1 and 7.2. Knowing what is effective is important since, in reality, "wish-lists" are of relatively little value. It is unlikely that health budgets will increase dramatically in the near future and there is likely to be increased competition for funds (Clark 1985). Abel-Smith (1982, 177, 180) has noted that this is not an economic climate in which governments are likely to launch costly new programs to promote the welfare of the elderly. However, it has been said that a society should be judged according to what it does for its old people (Jackson 1985).

Moreover, increased expenditure may not do more than provide a partial solution. For example, the United States per capita expenditure on health care is almost four times that in the United Kingdom, but the United States allocation dilemmas are similar to those in Britain (Linton and Naylor 1985). It is better perhaps to think in terms of "trade-offs," which emphasize the need to establish priorities and cost-effectiveness. Moreover, in this connection, Zuckerman's remarks (1969, 32) are of importance for the elderly:

> No country can plan for the future without laying down priorities within the limit of the resources it has available. The social value of highly costly clinical developments which circumstances will confine to a few will have to be balanced against the benefits which all will enjoy if common ailments ... are made less troublesome than they now are ...

7.3.1 Careers in Long-Term Care

Gerontology is an emerging discipline, and there are advantages and disadvantages associated with this growth, including the question of whether gerontology should be regarded as an initial discipline or as a specialization following the basic professional training. However, given a genuine interest in the subject, a variety of individuals can find satisfying and worthwhile work in the area. On the one hand, a person with little formal academic background can play a useful role by becoming involved in various home-support systems. At the other end of the academic spectrum, there are numerous questions of considerable interest which can be investigated by qualified researchers in a number of disciplines. For example, in the medical area, it is hoped, as stated in a *Lancet* editorial (1986), that "we can attract the brains as well as the hearts of our medical students to the basic sciences of gerontology during their pre-clinical years."

The disadvantage of gerontology as an emerging area is that it is not yet well recognized, and the status of the gerontologist is not well established. It is hoped that gerontologists will be involved in programs which aim to prevent unnecessary institutionalization, and that individuals who have a multidisciplinary understanding of aging will be involved in the development of policy and in the implementation of programs concerning institutional care.

7.3.2 No Single Policy or Program Solution

On the basis of what has been said previously, it is evident that there is no single or global solution which has been judged to be appropriate for all the different regions of Canada. In fact, it is probably desirable that the various approaches which have evolved, and which involve different combinations of assistance, are maintained. In this way a number of options are available for consideration as program development occurs and as policies are being formulated. In other words, it is undesirable to strive for a uniform approach towards institutionalization of the elderly. Within existing fiscal constraints different policy and program approaches should be encouraged and then judged on the basis of their effectiveness.

It also seems appropriate that such experimentation should be undertaken mainly at the local or regional level. At the provincial or federal levels, and particularly in the larger provinces where there exists divided jurisdictional responsibility (see Section 6.8), it may be difficult to co-ordinate the activities of the different ministries involved, whereas this co-ordination may be easier at the local level. To illustrate, if a region were given funds that could be used for additional care beds, sheltered housing, or better home-support services, it is likely that at the local level trade-offs could be considered more easily between these and other alternatives. The provincial or federal agencies could provide options, the region could respond to these options, and the appropriate ministries could then either accept the proposal from the region, or return it with criticisms and suggestions for modification. In this way, a dialogue might ensure that local concerns and recommendations are incorporated, while the provincial or federal authorities can contribute the research expertise to assist with the evaluation. Thus, a mutually agreeable proposal could be developed.

7.4 THE FUTURE OF INSTITUTIONAL CARE

A Chinese proverb is purported to say, "To prophesy is extremely difficult – especially with respect to the future." Having sounded a word of caution about predictions, there is the question of how resources for the care of the elderly should be used in the future. An interesting illustration is the decision taken by the National Foundation for Infantile Paralysis in the 1940s and 1950s. It could at that time have invested most of its resources in producing better iron lungs. If that had been the case, today we would have perhaps the best and most comfortable iron lungs inhabited by polio victims. However, instead the foundation invested heavily in basic research to conquer polio and this proved to be the correct decision (Walford 1985).

Along these lines, one might argue that old age homes and vast support structures to care for the helpless aged represent the iron lungs of gerontology. They maintain the elderly, yet do not address the underlying problems. There are, of course, differences since the deterioration associated with old age is not entirely curable. However, the above-mentioned analogy is still relevant, particularly with respect to the dementias. Further improvements in support systems for the demented elderly may merely provide symptomatic relief for a problem which is likely to expand as the population ages, since dementias, particularly in persons who have no families available to provide support, generate an appreciable proportion of the need for institutional care. The alternative is that more efforts should be made to elucidate the risk factors for some of the dementias and other diseases which are prevalent among the elderly. This, in turn, raises the question of what would then happen to life expectancy.

7.4.1 Progress in the Prevention of Diseases Affecting the Elderly

Major diseases which now afflict the elderly are atherosclerosis, arthritis, senile dementias, and osteoporosis. The last few years have witnessed an increasing interest in the dementias, mainly because of the growing awareness of their prevalence and because of their importance in affecting the rates of institutionalization of the elderly. This area will therefore be discussed in some detail.

Dementing illnesses constitute an important contributing cause of death in developed countries. Moreover, the economic costs, particularly for nursing care, are heavy, and the emotional and social burden on families of demented persons can be devasting. It has been estimated that more than half of nursing home residents have some degree of intellectual impairment, while the prevalence of moderate and severe dementia in populations over sixty-five years of age is estimated to be about 7%,[1] of which up to half may reside in institutions. It seems that the proportion of dementia cases who are institutionalized (Preston 1986) is determined mainly by the number of available institutional beds. This has implications for the number of needed beds, and for the community services which could support such individuals at home.

There are reports that the prevalence of mental disorders depends on social class, on marital status and on place of birth (Halldin 1985). However, one of the problems of any survey is that individuals who participate in a survey may differ from those who do not. In the study by Halldin, there was a non-response rate of 12%. In analyzing the psychiatric diagnoses of "moderate and severe degree" of mental disorders, it was found that these were significantly more prevalent in the lower social class, where it was 14% and 2.7%, respectively, whereas in the upper class, prevalence was 6.9% and 0.6%. These percentages might be different if the non-respondents had been considered.[2]

Researchers are trying to identify risk factors for the various dementias. The need for longitudinal studies to provide information on age-specific incidence, and variation in incidence by sex, geographic location, ethnicity and other personal characteristics, is clear. Although longitudinal data have a number of difficulties associated with them (see Section 6.1.2), they represent a powerful tool, particularly since they provide the opportunity for intervention by assessing the value of a particular type of treatment. Unfortunately, studies of dementing illness are not easy to carry out because these diseases occur mainly in persons over seventy years of age when there may be difficulties getting accurate medical and social histories (Mortimer and Schuman 1981, 177). However, it has been hypothesized that head trauma (Mortimer et al. 1985), occupational environmental exposure to toxic agents, excessive use of alcohol and drugs, and nutritional factors (Abalan 1984) may play a part.

Current research into the dementias has considered not only the problem of diagnosis and of clinical care (Berger 1985; Council on Scientific Affairs 1986; Kohn 1985a, 1985b; Rango 1985), but also the underlying biological changes occurring in Alzheimer's disease (see, for example, Corbett 1985; Glenner 1985; Goldsmith 1985; Katzman 1986; Wurtman 1985). The problem of diagnosis is particularly important since the dementias include many different diseases, some of which are difficult to identify. As long as a disease cannot be identified, this will tend to inhibit progress. The problem of diagnosis is also important since it affects the estimates of numbers affected by the dementias (see note one). At present no effective treatment is possible for many organic dementias, but some trials involving drugs are being undertaken (Dehlin et al. 1985; Mizumori et al. 1985; Summers et al. 1986; Wettstein and Spiegel 1984).

Factors influencing the progress of other diseases which affect the elderly are receiving more attention (see, for example, Davies 1985; Lipschitz et al. 1985), and this, at least in part, is responsible for the decline in coronary and stroke death rates in many western countries over recent decades. Other conditions, such as urinary incontinence, are distressing to the elderly and may have major psychosocial, economic and physical consequences. Advances in diagnosis and the clinical management of diseases of the elderly are occurring (see Rowe 1985). The effect of psychosocial factors on health and longevity (see, for example, Rose and Bell 1971) is not clear, but is believed to be important; for example, individuals with lower income have considerably higher mortality rates.

7.4.2 Changes in Health Status and Life Span

The health status and average life span of the elderly will affect the number of institutionalized elderly. Several papers (see, for example, Fries 1980, 1984; Grundy 1984; Myers and Manton 1984) have addressed this question of predicting future mortality and morbidity and these papers raise a number of interesting points. Fries hypothesized a trend in which most people would have a relatively healthy life until an advanced age (over eighty-five) and then deteriorate and die rapidly before the assumed maximum life span. The implication is that in future, with this progressive "rectangularization" of the survival curve, there might be fewer people requiring institutional care. In the course of the twentieth century, such a trend in life expectancy has been apparent but it is not clear whether it will continue.

Information about mortality and its effects on the proportion of the population who are elderly is provided by the maximum human life span, the average life expectancy at specific ages, such as birth, forty-five, sixty-five, or eighty-five, and mortality rates at different ages. The average life expectancy and mortality rates are particularly important as far as health and social policies are concerned. For example, does prolonging life add to health costs? There are a number of issues which may affect the proportion of persons who will be institutionalized in the future, such as:

(a) Are there indications that the maximum life span has increased over-time?

(b) Are individuals who have reached a certain age, such as sixty-five, healthier now than they were some years ago?

(c) Can we expect people at age sixty-five to be healthier in future than the present cohort of such individuals?

(d) As more people live longer, will the very old require more or less care during the course of their remaining years?

Fries (1984) refers to a genetically determined life span and cites the observation that there is no conclusive evidence that anyone has died at a greater age than about one hundred and fifteen years. The evidence for an increase in the maximum life span has been reviewed critically by Schneider and Reed (1985) and Grundy (1984). Although we do not know whether the maximum human life span will increase, it is most likely that increases in average length of life will occur. Even if the maximum life span were not to increase appreciably, this may not be of great significance compared with the substantial increases in the number of people who survive to age eighty, eighty-five, ninety or ninety-five. Life expectancy even at age eighty-five and over has increased, if only slightly, during the last few years. The available information is provided by age-specific mortality rates, which have declined. If a trend towards rectangularization were occurring, not only would mortality rates for most age-groups be decreasing, which has been happening, but also the mortality rate for the oldest age-groups would be increasing in order to remove the larger number of survivors as the assumed maximum life span is reached. In fact, the mortality of the oldest age-group, that is those over age eighty-five, has not only been decreasing, but has been doing so faster than those in the age-groups fifty-five to sixty-four, sixty-five to seventy-four or seventy-five to eighty-four, at least in the United States (see Brody 1985; Schneider and Brody 1983; for Canadian data see Stone and Fletcher 1986).

Moreover, if the survival curve were to move towards rectangularization, this may not ensure a compression of morbidity, because people may be incurring chronic diseases at similar ages as at present, and merely survive longer because they receive more effective medical care. Schneider and Brody (1983) believe that there is no evidence of declining morbidity or disability in any age-group, and particularly not in the forty-five to sixty-four age-group. Manton (1986) has investigated specific causes of mortality and has found no significant changes in these occurrences between 1968 and 1980. On the other hand, a Swedish study (Svanborg et al. 1983) which investigated successive cohorts on reaching their seventieth birthday, concluded that the 1982–83 cohort had more healthy hearts, lungs and kidneys than the cohort examined in 1971–72. Palmore (1986) reports similar results in the United States. These latter reports would provide support for Fries' contention regarding compression of morbidity.

The question of whether individuals at age sixty-five are healthier now than in the past, like the question of a maximum human life span, cannot be answered therefore with certainty. It will depend on what is meant by "healthier" or "fitter." If we assume as a first approximation that mortality is related to morbidity (but see above), it may be noted that mortality rates at age sixty-five and over have decreased, suggesting that the present cohort of individuals who reached age sixty-five are probably healthier than those who reached that same age twenty or thirty years ago. Similarly, in attempting to make predictions for the future, there is evidence that mortality rates from major diseases such as heart disease and other clinical manifestations of arteriosclerosis, are decreasing. This suggests that, since these causes represent the majority of deaths and considerable morbidity, current all-cause mortality rates will continue to decline, and elderly individuals will be healthier. In fact, there is evidence that the average age of persons in chronic care facilities has increased (see Section 3.2). This suggests that the health of the elderly population has improved and consequently people, on average, are older before thay require institutionalization.

7.4.3 Other Issues Affecting the Future of Institutional Care

In the past, physicians were trained to diagnose the problems of patients, to treat them in the best possible manner using available medical skills and technology, and not to be overly concerned with economic or business aspects. Implicitly, quality was considered more important than quantity, generally and also as it concerned institutionalization. Many believe that this position should not be compromised (Soffer 1985; see also Naylor and Linton 1986). Yet, at the same time, economic considerations (Thurow 1985) will presumably exert a greater influence in the provision of health care as costs escalate. Long-term institutional care currently uses a much larger proportion of health-care funds than community-support services. The distribution of resources is complicated since a number of agencies, both private and government (for example, Health and Welfare Canada and Canada Mortgage and Housing Corporation at the federal level, and provincial departments of health, housing and social services), are involved in providing services for the elderly. Such fragmentation is associated with additional available options but may be not only confusing but also costly. Nevertheless it has been suggested (Freedman 1985) that, if current trends continue, the major parties involved in the purchase of health care will be the government or private business enterprises (see also *Lancet* 1985b). Together they can be expected to own, finance, organize, deliver and compete for the management of the various forms of health care. Presumably these organizations will aim to make the services offered, including institutionalization, as cost-effective as possible, bearing in mind that there is considerable debate about the meaning of cost-effectiveness (Avorn 1984; Doubilet et al. 1986; and see Section 6.9). Of particular importance may be the development of incentives which would provide financial rewards to institutions or organizations offering affordable care.

7.5 SUMMARY AND CONCLUSIONS

The previous chapter identified sources of discontent regarding the current state of knowledge about institutional care of the elderly. The aim of the present chapter is to consider future directions for policy and research. The material covered in this chapter stresses what might be done to improve quality of care for the institutionalized elderly through appropriate research. It is recognized that on the basis of present knowledge, there is no simple solution to many of the problems discussed.

This chapter also considers the future of institutional care and emphasizes that many aspects of this care will depend on progress made in preventing or alleviating diseases of old age, especially senile dementias. The effect of such progress on the average life span is also outlined. There are a number of questions to which we do not know the answers. These include whether the aged are now healthier than were their predecessors, and whether prevention and various social support programs have the potential to prolong good health and independence among the expanding elderly population (see Tulchinsky et al. 1985).

The following may be concluded:

1. There are many investigations which could be carried out to improve the quality, and outcome, of programs of care. Some of the more urgent questions concern: excessive medication; the role of physicians, nurses and others involved in institutional care; segregation of patients; palliative care; the various home-support systems; housing; the role of the family; inappropriate data

bases; staffing problems; predictors of institutionalization; and, preventive actions.

2. Present knowledge does not permit us, in many cases, to identify a single or simple solution to many of the problems discussed and, partly because of the heterogeneity of the elderly population, such a solution may not be available or desirable.

3. The extent of services required will depend on the progress made in preventing or alleviating diseases and on the changes which occur in the average life span.

4. The senile dementias are of particular importance since their prevalence may be so great that institutionalization can only provide a partial solution. In addition, the economic costs and emotional and social burden on families of demented persons can be devastating.

5. The model suggested by Fries (1980, 1984), which implies that in the future most people will live until an advanced age and then deteriorate rapidly, and that consequently there would be relatively fewer people requiring institutional care, is regarded as overly optimistic.

6. It is predicted that economic considerations will exert a greater influence on long-term care institutions.

NOTES

1. A survey of institutions in the Kingston area identified 628 elderly residents with significant dementia living in the institutions surveyed. According to the 1981 census, there was a population of 15,651 over age sixty-five in that area, suggesting that 4% of that population were institutionalized persons with significant dementia. An unknown, but probably low, proportion of the numerator figure had been residents of other districts prior to institutionalization, which would increase the rate slightly. However, compensating for this are the one or two small institutions which did not participate in the survey. The observed rate might also be slightly lower than the true rate because the data in the numerator were obtained one year earlier than the data for the denominator (see Proposal for an Integrated Community Project on the Care of the Elderly Persons with Dysfunctional Brain Syndrome in the area of Kingston, Ontario, November 1981, submitted to the Ontario Ministries of Health and of Community and Social Services). However, since many demented elderly are cared for at home, the overall prevalence of dementia in the sixty-five and over age group is probably several times higher than the above-mentioned rate of 4%. An estimate that about

25% of those with dementia live in institutions and 75% live at home was derived from five surveys which reported place of residence (Kay and Bergmann 1980, 44). Based on these data, a reasonable estimate of the prevalence of all degrees of dementia in the sixty-five and over group would be 4 × 4% or 16%; other studies suggest even higher rates (Häfner 1985; Mortimer and Schuman 1981, 5–10; Peace 1984, 87–90; Pfeffer et al. 1987; Preston 1986).

2. It should be noted that the data of Halldin (1985) indicate associations but do not establish a cause-and-effect relationship. In other words, it is not known whether a lower social class leads to a higher prevalence of "moderate" and "severe" psychiatric illness, or if the presence of these conditions, or their precursors, have led to individuals being located among the lower social classes, or whether some confounding variables lead to both the psychiatric condition and to an individual being in the lower social class. Another confounding variable may be a class difference in seeking medical attention for this condition. Although not establishing cause and effect, longitudinal data would clarify the temporal relationship since they would be able to show whether lower social class precedes a mental disorder, or whether signs of mental disorder precede the placement of the individual in a lower social class.

BIBLIOGRAPHY

Abalan, F.
   1984   "Alzheimer's Disease and Malnutrition: A New Etiological Hypothesis."
           Medical Hypotheses 15:385–93.
Abel-Smith, B.
   1960   *A History of the Nursing Profession*. London: Heinemann Educational
           Books Ltd.
Abel-Smith, B.
   1982   "Economic Commentary." In P. Selby and M. Schechter. *Aging 2000: A
           Challenge for Society*. Lancaster, U.K.: MTP Press, 1977–86.
Agnew, G. H.
   1974   *Canadian Hospitals, 1920–1970. A Dramatic Half-Century*. Toronto:
           University of Toronto Press.
Aiken, L. H.
   1986   "Evaluation Research and Public Policy: Lessons from the National
           Hospice Study." *Journal of Chronic Diseases* 39(1):1–4.
Allen, C. M., P. M. Becker, L. J. McVey, et al.
   1986   "A Randomized, Controlled Clinical Trial of a Geriatric Consultation
           Team." *Journal of the American Medical Association* 255(19):2617–21.
Anderson, Sir F., and B. Williams
   1983   *Practical Management of the Elderly*. Fourth Edition. Oxford: Blackwell
           Scientific Publications.
Andrews, K.
   1985   "Demographic Changes and Resources for the Elderly." *British Medical
           Journal* 290(6474):1023–24.
Andrews, K., M. A. Harding, and D. Goldstone
   1985   "Social Implications of Multiple Pathology." *Gerontology* 31(5):325–31.
Arie, T.
   1977   "Issues in the Psychiatric Care of the Elderly." In A. N. Exton-Smith and
           J. Grimley Evans (eds.). *Care of the Elderly: Meeting the Challenge of
           Dependency*. London: Academic Press; New York: Grune and Stratton,
           67–80.
Aronson, J.
   1985   "Family Care of the Elderly: Underlying Assumptions and Their Conse-
           quences." *Canadian Journal on Aging* 4(3):115–25.
Aronson, M. K.
   1984   "Implementing a Teaching Nursing Home: Lessons for Research and
           Practice." *The Gerontologist* 24(5):451–54.
Ashley, M.J., C.I. Gryfe, and A. Amies
   1977   "A Longitudinal Study of Falls in an Elderly Population. II. Some Cir-
           cumstances of Falling." *Age and Ageing* 6:211–20.

Avorn, J.
  1984   "Benefit and Cost Analysis in Geriatric Care." *The New England Journal of Medicine* 310(20):1294-301.
Barbieri, E. B.
  1983   "Patient Falls Are Not Patient Accidents." *Journal of Gerontological Nursing* 9(3):165-73.
Bayer, R., D. Callahan, J. Fletcher, et al.
  1983   "The Care of the Terminally Ill: Morality and Economics." *The New England Journal of Medicine* 309(24):1490-94.
Bayne, J. R. D., and J. Caygill
  1977   "Identifying Needs and Services for the Aged." *Journal of the American Geriatrics Society* 25(6):264-68.
Beattie, W. M. Jr.
  1976   "Aging and the Social Services." In R. H. Binstock and E. Shanas (eds.). *Handbook of Aging and the Social Sciences*. New York: Van Nostrand Reinhold Co., 619-42.
Béland, F.
  1986   "The Clientele of Comprehensive and Traditional Home Care Programs." *The Gerontologist* 26(4):382-88.
Bentkover, J. D., F. A. Sloan, F. G. Feeley, et al.
  1984   "Hospital Capital and Operating Costs." In R. M. Scheffler and L. F. Rossiter (eds.). *Advances in Health Economics and Health Services Research* (Vol. 5). Greenwich, Conn.: JAI Press Inc., 213-36.
Berg, R. L., F. E. Browning, J. G. Hill, and W. Wenkert
  1970   "Assessing the Health Care Needs of the Aged." *Health Services Research* 5:36-59.
Berger, E. Y.
  1985   "The Institutionalization of Patients with Alzheimer's Disease." *Danish Medical Bulletin* 32(1):71-76.
Berk, M. L., and G. R. Wilensky
  1985   "Health Care of the Poor Elderly: Supplementing Medicare." *The Gerontologist* 25(3):311-14.
Berrey, P. N. E.
  1986   "Increase in Acute Admissions and Death after Closing a Geriatric Day Hospital." *British Medical Journal* 292(Jan. 18):176-78.
Berry, G., R. H. Fisher, and S. Lang
  1981   "Detrimental Incidents, Including Falls, in an Elderly Institutional Population." *Journal of the American Geriatrics Society* 29(7):322-24.
Bloom, B. S., R. S. Knorr, and A. E. Evans
  1985   "The Epidemiology of Disease Expenses." *Journal of the American Medical Association* 253(16):2393-97.
Blum, S. R., and M. Minkler
  1980   "Toward a Continuum of Caring Alternatives: Community Based Care for the Elderly." *Journal of Social Issues* 36(2):133-52.
Booth, T.
  1985   *Home Truths. Old People's Homes and the Outcome of Care*. Aldershot, England and Brookfield, Vt., U.S.A.: Gower Publishing Company.

Borup, J. H.
  1981   "Relocation: Attitudes, Information Network and Problems Encountered." *The Gerontologist* 21(5):501–11.
Bowman, B. B., and I. H. Rosenberg
  1982   "Assessment of the Nutritional Status of the Elderly." *American Journal of Clinical Nutrition* 35:1142–51.
Branch, L. G., and A. M. Jette
  1982   "A Prospective Study of Long-Term Care Institutionalization Among the Aged." *American Journal of Public Health* 72:1373–79.
Branch, L. G., and A. M. Jette
  1984   "Personal Health Practices and Mortality Among the Elderly." *American Journal of Public Health* 74(10):1126–29.
Brink, C. J.
  1985   "Drugs are Cost Effective, says PMA Report." *American Journal of Hospital Pharmacy* 42(4):718–28.
Brocklehurst, J. C.
  1977   "Inculcation of Appropriate Attitudes and Skills." In A. N. Exton-Smith and J. Grimley Evans (eds.). *Care of the Elderly: Meeting the Challenge of Dependency*. London: Academic Press; New York: Grune and Stratton, 234–41.
Brocklehurst, J. C. (ed.)
  1984   *Urology in the Elderly*. Edinburgh: Churchill Livingstone.
Brocklehurst, J. C. (ed.)
  1985   *Textbook of Geriatric Medicine and Gerontology*. Third Edition. Edinburgh: Churchill Livingstone.
Brody, E. M.
  1977(a) *Long-term Care of Older People. A Practical Guide*. New York and London: Human Sciences Press.
Brody, E. M.
  1977(b) "Environmental Factors in Dependency." In A. N. Exton-Smith and J. Grimley Evans (eds.). *Care of the Elderly: Meeting the Challenge of Dependency*. London: Academic Press; New York: Grune and Stratton, 81–95.
Brody, E. M.
  1981   " 'Women in the Middle' and Family Help to Older People." *The Gerontologist* 21(5):471–80.
Brody, E. M., H. Kleban, and M. Moss
  1974   "Measuring the Impact of Change." *The Gerontologist* 14:299–305.
Brody, E. M., and C. B. Schoonover
  1986   "Patterns of Parent-Care When Adult Daughters Work and When They Do Not." *The Gerontologist* 26(4):372–81.
Brody, J. A.
  1985   "Prospects for an Ageing Population." *Nature*; 315 (June 6): 463–66.
Burgio, K. L., W. E. Whitehead, and B. T. Engel
  1985   "Urinary Incontinence in the Elderly. Bladder-Sphincter Biofeedback and Toileting Skills Training." *Annals of Internal Medicine* 130(4): 507–15.
Canada, Dominion Bureau of Statistics
  1944   *The Canada Year Book 1943–44*. Ottawa, Ontario.

Canada, Dominion Bureau of Statistics
  1954   *The Canada Year Book 1954.* Ottawa, Ontario.
Canada, Dominion Bureau of Statistics
  1964   *The Canada Year Book 1963–64.* Ottawa, Ontario.
Canada Mortgage and Housing Corporation
  1979   *Nursing Homes and Hostels With Care Services for the Elderly. Design Guidelines.* Ottawa, Ontario: Canada Mortgage and Housing Corporation.
Canadian Council on Homemaker Services
  1982   *Visiting Homemakers Services in Canada: Survey, 1982.* Toronto, Ontario.
Cape, R.
  1978   *Aging: Its Complex Management.* Hagerstown, Md.: Harper & Row.
Cape, R. D. T., C. Shorrock, R. Tree, et al.
  1977   "Square Pegs in Round Holes: A Study of Residents in Long-Term Institutions in London, Ontario." *Canadian Medical Association Journal* 117:1284–87.
Carp, F. M.
  1980   "Effects of the Living Environment on Activity and Use of Time." In J. Hendricks (ed.). *Institutionalization and Alternative Futures.* Perspectives on Aging and Human Development Series; 3. Farmingdale, New York: Baywood Publishing Company, Inc., 92–108.
Cantor, M. H.
  1983   "Strain Among Caregivers: A Study of Experience in the United States." *The Gerontologist* 23(6):597–604.
Catchen, H.
  1983   "Repeaters: Inpatient Accidents Among the Hospitalized Elderly." *The Gerontologist* 23(3):273–76.
Chambers, L. W., E. A. Mohide, J. R. D. Bayne, et al.
  1983   "A Self-monitoring Method of Resident Care Quality Assurance in Long Term Care Facilities." *Canadian Journal on Aging* 2(3):137–51.
Chappell, N. L.
  1985   "Social Support and the Receipt of Home Care Services." *The Gerontologist* 25(1):47–54.
Chappell, N. L., and B. Havens
  1985   "Who Helps the Elderly Person: A Discussion of Formal and Informal Care." In W. A. Peterson and J. Quadagno (eds.). *Social Bonds in Later Life. Aging and Interdependence.* Beverly Hills, London, New Delhi: Sage Publications, 211–27.
Chappell, N. L., L. A. Strain, and A. A. Blandford
  1986   *Aging and Health Care. A Social Perspective.* Toronto, Ontario: Holt, Rinehart and Winston of Canada, Ltd.
Clarfield, A. M.
  1983   "Home Care: Is it Cost-Effective?" *Canadian Medical Association Journal* 129:1181–83; 1199.
Clark, P. G.
  1985   "The Social Allocation of Health Care Resources: Ethical Dilemmas in Age-Group Competition." *The Gerontologist* 125(2):119–25.

Clark, S. D.
1942   *The Social Development of Canada. An Introductory Study With Select Documents*. Toronto, Ontario: The University of Toronto Press.
Clarke-Williams, M. J.
1983   "Ward Furniture and Equipment." In M. J. Denham (ed.). *Care of the Long-Stay Elderly Patient*. London and Canberra: Croom Helm Ltd., 71–89.
Collings, T.
1985   "Demographic Changes and Resources for the Elderly." *British Medical Journal* 290 (April 27): 1284.
Comfort, A.
1980   *Practice of Geriatric Psychiatry*. New York: Elsevier North Holland, Inc.
Commonwealth of Australia
1979   *Rehabilitation in Health Services*. Monograph Series No. 6. Canberra: Commonwealth of Australia, Commonwealth Dept. of Health (Policy and Planning Division).
Connidis, I.
1983   "Living Arrangement Choices of Older Residents: Assessing Quantitative Results with Qualitative Data. *The Canadian Journal of Sociology* 8(4):359–75.
Connidis, I.
1985   "The Service Needs of Older People: Implications for Public Policy." *Canadian Journal on Aging* 4(1):3–10.
Coons, D. H.
1983   "The Therapeutic Milieu: Social-Psychological Aspects of Treatment." In W. Reichel (ed.). *Clinical Aspects of Aging*. Second Edition. Baltimore/London: Williams and Wilkins, 137–50.
Corbett, J. A.
1985   "Ageing and Mental Retardation — A New Challenge." *Journal of the Royal Society of Medicine* 78(2):166–68.
Council on Scientific Affairs, Chicago
1986   "Dementia." *Journal of the American Medical Association* 256(16): 2234–38.
Crooks, J., K. O'Malley, and I. H. Stevenson
1976   "Pharmacokinetics in the Elderly." *Clinical Pharmacokinetics* 1:280–96.
Cullen, M. F.
1983   "Nursing Care." In M. J. Denham (ed.). *Care of the Long-Stay Elderly Patient*. London and Canberra: Croom Helm Ltd., 42–70.
Curry, T. J., and B. W. Ratliff
1973   "The Effect of Nursing Home Size on Resident Isolation and Life Satisfaction." *The Gerontologist* 13(3):295–98.
Davies, A. M.
1985   "Empidemiology and the Challenge of Ageing." *International Journal of Epidemiology* 14(1):9–21.
Dehlin, O., B. Hedenrud, P. Jansson, and J. Nörgard
1985   "A Double-blind Comparison of Alaproclate and Placebo in the Treatment of Patients with Senile Dementia." *Acta Psychiatrica Scandinavica* 71(2):190–96.

Denham, M. J. (ed.)
  1983   *"Care of the Long-Stay Elderly Patient."* London and Canberra: Croom
          Helm Ltd.
Dobrof, R., J. M. Metsch, H. R. Moody, et al.
  1980   "The Long-Term Care Challenge: Rationalizing A Continuum of Care
          for Chronically Impaired Elderly." *Mount Sinai Journal of Medicine*
          47(2):87–95.
Doepel, L. K.
  1985   "Looking at Menopause's Role in Osteoporosis." *Journal of the
          American Medical Association* 254(17):2379–80.
Doherty, N. J. G., and B. C. Hicks
  1975   "The Use of Cost-Effectiveness Analysis in Geriatric Day Care." *The
          Gerontologist* 15(5, 1):412–17.
Doubilet, P., M. C. Weinstein, and B. J. McNeil
  1986   "Use and Misuse of the Term 'Cost Effective' in Medicine." *The New
          England Journal of Medicine* 314(4):253–56.
Draper, C. L. W.
  1985   "More Comprehensive Institutional Geriatric Services." *Canadian Med-
          ical Association Journal* 132(4):322.
Dulude, L.
  1978   *Women and Aging: A Report on the Rest of our Lives.* Ottawa,
          Ontario: Canadian Advisory Council on the Status of Women.
Edelson, J. S., and W. H. Lyons
  1985   *Institutional Care of the Mentally Impaired Elderly.* New York: Van
          Nostrand Reinhold Company.
Eisdorfer, C.
  1977   "Mental Health Problems in the Aged." In A. N. Exton-Smith and
          J. Grimley Evans (eds.). *Care of the Elderly: Meeting the Challenge of
          Dependency.* London: Academic Press; New York: Grune and Stratton,
          59–67.
Elliot, J. R.
  1975   *Living in Hospital.* London: King Edward's Hospital Fund.
Emodi, B.
  1977   *Programs and Services in Nursing Homes and Hostels.* Working Paper
          No. 3. CMHC Nursing Home and Hostels Design Guidelines Study.
          Ottawa, Ontario: Canada Mortgage and Housing Corporation.
Evans, J. G.
  1977   "Current Issues in the United Kingdom." In A. N. Exton-Smith and
          J. Grimley Evans (eds.). *Care of the Elderly: Meeting the Challenge of
          Dependency.* London: Academic Press; New York: Grune and Stratton,
          130–32.
Extended Health Care Services Program
  1981   Ottawa, Health Services and Promotion Branch, Health and Welfare
          Canada.
Factor, H., and J. Habib
  1985   "Role of Institutional and Community Services in Meeting the Long-
          Term Care Needs of the Elderly in Israel: the Decade of the 1980s."
          Israel Journal of Medical Sciences 21:212–18.

Feil, N.
    1982   *V/F, Validation. The Feil Method. How to Help Disoriented Old-Old.*
            Cleveland, Ohio: Edward Feil Productions.
Finland. Ministry of Social Affairs and Health
    1982   *Aging in Finland. Finnish National Report for the World Assembly on*
            Aging. Helsinki: Ministry of Social Affairs and Health.
Fischer, D. H.
    1978   *Growing Old in America. The Blanch-Lee Lectures delivered at Clark*
            University. Expanded Edition. Oxford: Oxford University Press.
Fisher, R. H., and M. L. Zorzitto
    1983   "Placement Problem: Diagnosis, Disease or Term of Denigration?"
            Canadian Medical Association Journal 129:331–34.
Fottler, M. D., H. L. Smith, and W. L. James
    1981   "Profits and Patient Care Quality in Nursing Homes: Are They Com-
            patible?" *The Gerontologist* 21(5):532–38.
Frampton, D. R.
    1986   "Restoring Creativity to the Dying Patient." *British Medical Journal*
            293(6562):1593–95.
Freedman, S. A.
    1985   "Megacorporate Health Care. A Choice for the Future." *The New*
            England Journal of Medicine 312(9):579–82.
Freedman, D., R. Pisani, and R. Purves
    1978   *Statistics.* New York and London: W. W. Norton and Company.
Fries, J. F.
    1980   "Aging, Natural Death, and the Compression of Morbidity." *The New*
            England Journal of Medicine 303(3):130–35.
Fries, J. F.
    1984   "The Compression of Morbidity: Miscellaneous Comments About a
            Theme." *The Gerontologist* 24(4):354–59.
Fryer, M. L., and F. G. Piercey
    1981   *Towards Meeting the Needs of Senior Citizens in Prince Edward Island.*
            Survey of Senior Citizens: Characteristics, Needs, Resources. Prince
            Edward Island: Department of Health and Social Services, Social
            Resources Branch, Special Services Division.
Gelber, S. M.
    1980   "The Path to Health Insurance." In C. A. Meilicke and J. L. Storch
            (eds.). *Perspectives on Canadian Health and Social Services Policy: His-*
            tory and Emerging Trends. Ann Arbor, Michigan: Health Administra-
            tion Press, School of Public Health, University of Michigan, 156–65.
Gentleman, J. F., K. S. Brown, and W. F. Forbes
    1978   "Smoking and its Effect on Mortality of the Elderly." *The American*
            Journal of Medical Sciences 276(2):173–83.
Gerson, L. W., and O. P. Hughes
    1976   "A Comparative Study of the Economics of Home Care." *International*
            Journal of Health Services 6(4):543–55.
Gibson, M. J.
    1984   "Family Support Patterns, Policies and Programs." In C. Nusberg.
            Innovative Aging Programs Abroad. Implications for the United States.
            Westport, Connecticut: Greenwood Press, 159–95.

Gilleard, C. J.
    1985   "Predicting the Outcome of Psychogeriatric Day Care." *The Gerontologist* 25(3):280–85.
Ginsberg, G. M.
    1985   "Balance of Care in Services to the Elderly in Israel." *Israel Journal of Medical Sciences* 21:230–37.
Glenner, G. G.
    1985   "On Causative Theories in Alzheimer's Disease." *Human Pathology* 16(5):433–35.
Glosser, G., and D. Wexler
    1985   "Participants' Evaluation of Educational/Support Groups for Families of Patients with Alzheimer's Disease and Other Dementias." *The Gerontologist* 25(3):232–36.
Goffman, E.
    1961   *Asylums. Essays on the Social Situation of Mental Patients and Other Inmates*. Garden City, N.Y.: Anchor Books, Doubleday and Company, Inc.
Goldsmith, M. F.
    1985   "Research on aging burgeons as more Americans grow older." *The Journal of American Medical Association* 253(10):1369–1405.
Gordon, M.
    1982   "Falls in the Elderly: More Common, More Dangerous." *Geriatrics* 37(4):117–20.
Gorrod, J. W.
    1974   "Absorption, Metabolism and Excretion of Drugs in Geriatric Subjects." *Gerontologia Clinica* 16:30–42.
Gosney, M., and R. Tallis
    1984   "Prescription of Contraindicated and Interacting Drugs in Elderly Patients Admitted to Hospital." *The Lancet II*:564–67.
Grant, P. R.
    1985(a) "Who Experiences the Move into a Nursing Home as Stressful? Examination of the Relocation Stress Hypothesis Using Archival, Time-Series Data." *Canadian Journal on Aging* 4(2):87–100.
Grant, P. R.
    1985(b) "Predictors of the Level of Care Assigned to New Nursing Home Residents." *Canadian Journal on Aging* 4(1):38–46.
Grauer, H.
    1985   "Restraints and the Elderly." Letter to the Editor. *Canadian Medical Association Journal* 133:556.
Gray, B. H. (ed.)
    1986   *For-profit Enterprise in Health Care*. Washington, D.C.: Academy Press.
Gray, J. A. M.
    1985   *Prevention of Disease in the Elderly*. Edinburgh and New York: Churchill Livingstone.
Greenblatt, D. J., M. D. Allen, and R. I. Shader
    1977   "Toxicity of High-Dose Flurazepam in the Elderly." *Clincal Pharmacology and Therapeutics* 21(3):355–61.

Greenfield, W. L.
   1984   "Disruption and Reintegration: Dealing with Familial Response to Nurs-
          ing Home Placement." *Journal of Gerontological Social Work* 8(1/2):
          15–21.
Greenwald, S. R., and M. W. Linn
   1971   "Intercorrelation of Data on Nursing Homes." *The Gerontologist* 11(4):
          337–40.
Greer, D. S., and V. Mor
   1986   "An Overview of National Hospice Study Findings." *Journal of Chronic
          Diseases* 39(1):5–7.
Greer, D. S., V. Mor, J. N. Morris, et al.
   1986   "An Alternative in Terminal Care: Results of the National Hospice
          Study." *Journal of Chronic Diseases* 39(1):9–26.
Grob, D.
   1983   "Prevalent Joint Diseases in Older Persons." In W. Reichel (ed.). *Clincal
          Aspects of Aging*. Second Edition. Baltimore/London: Williams and
          Wilkins, 344–59.
Gross, M. J., and C. W. Schwenger
   1981   *Health Care Costs for the Elderly in Ontario 1976–2026*. Toronto:
          Ontario Economic Council.
Grundy, E.
   1984   "Mortality and Morbidity Among the Old." *British Medical Journal*
          288:663–64.
Grundy, E., and T. Arie
   1984   "Institutionalization and the Elderly: International Comparisons." *Age
          and Ageing* 13:129–37.
Gryfe, C. I.
   1983   "Falling and its Clinical Assessment." *Medicine North America* (July)
          2nd Series, No. 1:51–55.
Gryfe, C. I., A. Amies, and M. J. Ashley
   1977   "A Longitudinal Study of Falls in an Elderly Population: I. Incidence
          and Morbidity." *Age and Ageing* 6:201–10.
Gutman, G. M. and N. K. Blackie (eds.)
   1986   *Aging in Place: Housing Adaptations and Options for Remaining in the
          Community*. Burnaby, B.C.: The Gerontology Research Centre, Simon
          Fraser University.
Guttmacher, S., M. Teitelman, G. Chapin, G. Garbowski, and P. Schnall
   1981   "Ethics and Preventive Medicine: The Case of Borderline Hyper-
          tension." *Hastings Centre Report* 11(1):12–20.
Hadlock, D. C.
   1985   "The Hospice: Intensive Care of a Different Kind." *Seminars in Oncol-
          ogy* 12(4):357–67.
Häfner, H.
   1985   "Mental Disorder in Old Age — Medical and Social Risk Factors."
          Pharmacopsychiatry 18(1):6–9.
Halldin, J.
   1985   "Prevalence of Mental Disorder in an Urban Population in Central
          Sweden in Relation to Social Class, Marital Status and Immigration."
          Acta Psychiatrica Scandinavica 71(2):117–27.

Hamilton-Wentworth Placement Coordination Service, Ontario
    1985   *Annual Report of the Placement Coordination Service 1984-85.*
Havens, B.
    1986   "Boundary Crossing: An Organizational Challenge for Community-
            Based Long-Term Care Service Agencies." In A. O. Pelham,
            W. F. Clark (eds.). *Managing Home Care for the Elderly. Lessons from
            Community-Based Agencies.* New York: Springer Publishing Co.,
            77-98.
Health and Welfare Canada
    1982   *The Manitoba/Canada Home Care Study. An Overview of the Results.*
            Ottawa, Ontario: Dept. of National Health and Welfare; Policy, Plan-
            ning and Information Branch (April).
Heikkinen, E., W. E. Waters, and Z. J. Brzeziński
    1983   *The Elderly in Eleven Countries. A Sociomedical Survey.* Copenhagen,
            Denmark: The World Health Organization.
Hoaken, P. C. S.
    1985   "Restraints and the Elderly." Letter to the Editor. *Canadian Medical
            Association Journal* 133:556.
Hoffbrand, B. I.
    1985   "Geriatrics and Admission Policies." *The Lancet I* (8435):984.
Holliday, P., G. R. Fernie, B. E. Maki, and F. S. Lauzon
    1985   "Some Bioengineering Approaches to the Falling Problem." *Geriatric
            Medicine*, July, 1:161-64.
Hood, N. A.
    1976   "Urinary Incontinence." *Health Bulletin* 34:354-58.
Hu, T-w., L-f. Huang, and W. S. Cartwright
    1986   "Evaluation of the Costs of Caring for the Senile Demented Elderly: A
            Pilot Study." *The Gerontologist* 26(2):158-63.
Hussar, D. A.
    1985   "Drug Interactions in Geriatric Drug Use." In S. R. Moore and
            T. W. Teal (eds.). *Geriatric Drug Use — Clinical and Social Perspec-
            tives.* Toronto: Pergamon Press, 135-43.
Ingman, S. R., I. R. Lawson, P. G. Pierpaoli, and P. Blake
    1975   "A Survey of the Prescribing and Administration of Drugs in a Long-
            Term Care Institution for the Elderly." *Journal of the American Geri-
            atric Society* 23(7):309-16.
Iglehart, J. K.
    1986   "Canada's Health Care System." *The New England Journal of Medicine*
            315(3):202-8.
Jackson, J.A.
    1983   "Cause of Death in Very Old People." *Journal of the American Medical
            Association* 249(19):2637.
Jackson, J. A., and W. F. Forbes
    1986   *A Survey of the Elderly in the Waterloo Region.* Waterloo Region Social
            Resources Council.
Jackson, P. M.
    1985   "Economics of an Aging Population." *Journal of Epidemiology and
            Community Health* 39(2):97-101.

Jewett, M. A. S., G. R. Fernie, P. J. Holliday, and M. E. Pim
  1981   "Urinary Dysfunction in a Geriatric Long-Term Care Population: Prevalence and Patterns." *Journal of the American Geriatrics Society* 29(5):211–14.
Johnson, L. A.
  1973   *History of the Country of Ontario 1615–1875.* Whitby, Ontario: The Corporation of the County of Ontario.
Jolley, D., P. Smith, L. Billington, et al.
  1982   "Developing a Psychogeriatric Service." In D. Coakley (ed.). *Establishing a Geriatric Service.* London and Canberra: Croom Helm Ltd., 149–65.
Kaban, L., and J. Block
  1984   "Variations Between a Day Hospital's Team Assessments and Needs Perceived by Referral Source." *Canadian Journal on Aging* 3(3):147–50.
Kane, R. A., and R. L. Kane
  1981   *Assessing the Elderly: A Practical Guide to Measurement.* Lexington, Massachusetts: D. C. Heath and Co.
Kane, R. L., and R. A. Kane (eds.)
  1982   *Values and Long-Term Care.* Lexington, Massachusetts: D. C. Heath and Co.
Kane, R. L., and R. A. Kane
  1985(a) *A Will and a Way. What the United States Can Learn From Canada about Caring for the Elderly.* New York: Columbia University Press.
Kane, R. A., and R. L. Kane
  1985(b) "The Feasibility of Universal Long-Term Care Benefits: Ideas from Canada." *The New England Journal of Medicine* 312(21):1357–64.
Kasl, S. V.
  1972   "Physical and Mental Health Effects of Involuntary Relocation and Institutionalization of the Elderly — a Review." *American Journal of Public Health* 62:377–84.
Katzman, R.
  1986   "Alzheimer's Disease." *The New England Journal of Medicine* 314(15): 964–73.
Kay, D. W. K., and K. Bergmann
  1980   "Epidemiology of Mental Disorders Among the Aged in the Community." In J. E. Birren and R. S. Sloane (eds.). *Handbook of Mental Health and Aging.* Englewood Cliffs, N.J.: Prentice-Hall, Inc., 34–56.
Kayser-Jones, J. S.
  1986   "Open-Ward Accommodation in a Long-Term Care Facility: The Elderly's Point of View." *The Gerontologist* 26(1):63–69.
Kent, D. P.
  1965   "Aging — Fact and Fancy." *The Gerontologist* 5(2):51–56, 111.
Kohn, J.
  1983   "Assessing the Elderly Patient." *Canadian Medical Association Journal* 129:1030–33.
Kohn, J.
  1985(a) "The Issue of Alzheimer's Care and Treatment." *Canadian Medical Association Journal* 132(7):867–70.

Kohn, J.
  1985(b) "Alzheimer's Conference Provokes Guarded Optimism." *Canadian Medical Association Journal* 132(9):1056–57.
Kohn, R. R.
  1982 "Cause of Death in Very Old People." *Journal of the American Medical Association* 247(20):2793–97.
Kramer, C. H., and J. R. Kramer
  1976 *Basic Principles of Long-Term Patient Care: Developing a Therapeutic Community*. Springfield, Illinois: Charles C. Thomas.
Kraus, A. S.
  1984 "The Burden of Care for Families of Elderly Persons with Dementia." *Canadian Journal on Aging* 3(1):45–51.
Kraus, A. S., and M. I. Armstrong
  1977 "Effect of Chronic Home Care on Admission to Institutions Providing Long-Term Care." *Canadian Medical Association Journal* 117:747–49.
Kraus, A. S., M. I. Armstrong, and B. Koski
  1982 "Chronic Home Care in Ontario: Five-Year Follow-Up." *Canadian Family Physician* 28:1531–37.
Kraus, A. S., R. A. Spasoff, E. J. Beattie, et al.
  1976(a) "Elderly Applicants to Long-Term Care Institutions: I. Their Characteristics, Health Problems, and State of Mind." *Journal of the American Geriatrics Society* 24(3):117–25.
Kraus, A. S., R. A. Spasoff, E. J. Beattie, et al.
  1976(b) "Elderly Applicants to Long-Term Care: II. The Application Process, Placement and Care Needs." *Journal of the American Geriatrics Society* 24(4):165–72.
Kroenke, K.
  1985 "Polypharmacy. Causes, Consequences, and Cure." *The American Journal of Medicine* 79(2):149–52.
Kuramoto, K., and S. Matsushita
  1985 "The Treatment of Mild Hypertension in the Elderly. A Prospective Study Using Multiple Regression Analysis." *Japanese Circulation Journal* 49(11):1144–50.
The Lancet
  1985(a) "Treatment of Hypertension in the Over-60s." (June 15):1369–70.
The Lancet
  1985(b) "Private Nursing Homes and the Old." (Dec. 14):1338–40.
The Lancet
  1986 "Geriatrics and the U.S.A." (Jan. 18):133–34.
Lang, C., and C. Shelton
  1982 *The Directory: Programs for Senior Citizens Across Canada*. Toronto, Ontario: Canadian Pensioners Concerned Inc. Ontario Division.
Latto, S. M.
  1982 "Managing the Care System." In F. Glendenning (ed.). *Care in the Community: Recent Research and Current Projects*. Stoke-on-Trent, England: Beth Johnson Foundation Publications.
Lawton, M. P., B. Patnaik, and M. H. Kleban
  1980 "The Ecology of Adaptation to a New Environment." In J. Hendricks

(ed.). *Institutionalization and Alternative Futures.* Perspectives on Aging and Human Development Series; 3. Farmingdale, New York: Baywood Publishing Company, Inc., 109–20.

Lemke, S., and R. H. Moos
1986 "Quality of Residential Settings for Elderly Adults." *Journal of Gerontology* 41(2):268–76.

Linton, A. L., and D. Naylor
1985 "Problems of Health Care in Canada." *The Medical Journal of Australia* (May 13): 142:556–58.

Lipschitz, D. A., S. Goldstein, R. Reis, et al.
1985 "Cancer in the Elderly: Basic Science and Clinical Aspects." *Annals of Internal Medicine* 102(2):218–28.

Longest, B. B. Jr.
1978 "An Empirical Analysis of the Quality/Cost Relationship." *Hospital and Health Services Administration* 23:20–35.

Mandelstam, D.
1980 *Incontinence and its Management.* London: Groom Helm Ltd.

Manton, K. G.
1986 "Cause Specific Mortality Patterns Amongst the Oldest Old: Multiple Cause of Death Trends 1968–1980." *Journal of Gerontology* 41(2): 282–89.

Matthews, A. M., J. A. Tindale, and J. E. Norris
1984 "The Facts on Aging Quiz: A Canadian Validation and Cross-Cultural Comparison." *Canadian Journal on Aging* 3(4):165–74.

McDaniel, S. A.
1986 *Canada's Aging Population.* Toronto, Ontario: Butterworths.

McGrother, C. W., C. M. Castleden, H. Duffin, and M. Clarke
1986 "Provision of Services for Incontinent Elderly People at Home." *Journal of Epidemiology and Community Health* 40:134–38.

McKim, W. A., and B. L. Mishara
1987 *Drugs and Aging.* Toronto, Ontario: Butterworths.

Miller, R. R.
1973 "Drug Surveillance Utilizing Epidemiologic Methods. A Report from the BCDSP." *American Journal of Hospital Pharmacy* 30:584–92.

Milne, J. S.
1976 "Prevalence of Incontinence in the Elderly Age Groups." In F. L. Willington (ed.). *Incontinence in the Elderly.* London: Academic Press, 9–21.

Milne, J. S., K. Hope, and J. Williamson
1970 "Variability in Replies to a Questionnaire on Symptoms of Physical Illness." *Journal of Chronic Diseases* 22:805–10.

Mirotznik, J., and A. P. Ruskin
1984 "Inter-Institutional Relocation and its Effect on Health." *The Gerontologist* 24(3):286–91.

Mitchell-Pedersen, L., L. Edmund, E. Fingerote, and C. Powell
1985 "Let's Untie the Elderly." OAHA Quarterly (October):10–14.

Mizumori, S. J. Y., T. A. Patterson, H. Sternberg, et al.
1985 "Effects of Dietary Choline on Memory and Brain Chemistry in Aged Mice." *Neurobiology of Aging* 6(1):51–56.

Moos, R. H.
   1974   *Evaluating Treatment Environments: A Social Ecological Approach.*
          New York: John Wiley and Sons.
Mor, V., C. E. Gutkin, and S. Sherwood
   1985   "The Cost of Residential Care Homes Serving Elderly Adults." *Journal
          of Gerontology* 40(2):164–71.
Mor, V., S. Sherwood, and C. Gutkin
   1986   "A National Study of Residential Care for the Aged." *The Gerontologist*
          26(4):405–17.
Morgan, J. S.
   1980   "Social Welfare Services in Canada." In C. A. Meilicke and J. L. Storch
          (eds.). *Perspectives on Canadian Health and Social Services Policy: His-
          tory and Emerging Trends.* Ann Arbor, Michigan: Health Administra-
          tion Press, School of Public Health, University of Michigan, 83–113.
Mortimer, J. A., L. R. French, J. T. Hutton, and L. M. Schuman
   1985   "Head Injury as a Risk Factor for Alzheimer's Disease." *Neurology*
          35(2):264–67.
Mortimer, J. A., and L. M. Schuman (eds.)
   1981   *The Epidemiology of Dementia.* Oxford: Oxford University Press.
Mulley, G.
   1981   "Stroke Rehabilitation: What are We all Doing?" In T. Arie (ed.).
          Health Care of the Elderly. London: Croom Helm Ltd., 23–41.
Myers, G. C., and K. G. Manton
   1984   "Compression of Mortality: Myth or Reality?" *The Gerontologist*
          24(4):346–53.
Myles, J. F.
   1980   "Institutionalizing the Elderly: A Critical Assessment of the Sociology
          of Total Institutions." In V. W. Marshall (ed.). *Aging in Canada. Social
          Perspectives.* Don Mills, Ontario: Fitzhenry and Whiteside Ltd.,
          257–68.
Naylor, D., and A. L. Linton
   1986   "Allocation of Health Care Resources: A Challenge for the Medical Pro-
          fession." *Canadian Medical Association Journal* 134(4):333–40.
Nocks, B. C., R. M. Learner, et al.
   1986   "The Effects of a Community-based Long Term Care Project on Nursing
          Home Utilization." *The Gerontologist* 26(2):150–57.
Norris, J. E., J. A. Tindale, and A. M. Matthews
   1987   "The Factor Structure of the Facts on Aging Quiz." *The Gerontologist*
          (in press).
Nusberg, C.
   1984   *Innovative Aging Programs Abroad. Implications for the United States.*
          Westport, Connecticut: Greenwood Press.
O'Brien, J. E., and G. F. Streib
   1977   *Evaluative Research on Social Programs for the Elderly.* Washington,
          D.C.: U. S. Department of Health, Education and Welfare, Office of
          Human Development. DHEW Publication No. (OHD) 77-20120.
Ontaio Association of Homes for the Aged
   1985   *Guide to Caring for the Mentally Impaired Elderly.* Toronto: Methuen
          Publications.

Ontario Council of Health
1978   *Health Care for the Aged. A Report of the Ontario Council of Health.*
       Toronto, Ontario.
Ontario Hospital Association
1980   *Guidelines for Long Term Care.* Toronto, Ontario.
O.M.A. Section on Geriatrics
1984   "O.M.A. Position Paper on Geriatric Medicine." Ontario Medical
       Review, October, 535–37.
Ontario Ministry of Health
1977   *Guidelines for Design of Chronic Care Units.* Toronto: Government of
       Ontario.
Ontario Ministry of Health
1980   *Patient Care Classification.* Toronto: Government of Ontario.
Ontario Ministry of Health
1985   *Information Resources and Services Branch,* Ontario.
Ontario Secretariat for Social Development
1981   *The Elderly in Ontario: An Agenda for the '80's.* Report of the Task
       Force on Aging. Toronto, Ontario.
Opit, L. J.
1977   "Domiciliary Care for the Elderly Sick — Economy or Neglect?" *British
       Medical Journal* 1(Jan. 1):30–33.
Ouslander, J. G., R. L. Kane, and I. B. Abrass
1982   "Urinary Incontinence in Elderly Nursing Home Patients." *Journal of
       the American Medical Association* 248(10):1194–98.
Pablo, R. Y.
1977(a) "Patient Accidents in a Long-Term-Care Facility." *Canadian Journal of
       Public Health* 68:237–47.
Pablo, R. Y.
1977(b) "Intra-Institutional Relocation: Its Impact on Long-Term Care
       Patients." *The Gerontologist* 17(5):426–35.
Palmore, E.
1977   "Facts on Aging: A Short Quiz." *The Gerontologist* 17(4):315–20.
Palmore, E. B.
1986   "Trends in the Health of the Aged." *The Gerontologist* 26(3):298–302.
Passmore, G. W.
1967   "Development of Homes for the Aged in Ontario." Unpublished type-
       script. Toronto: Department of Social and Family Services. (See also:
       N. Rudy, 1987. *For Such a Time as This. L. Earl Ludlow and the History
       of Homes for the Aged in Ontario, 1837–1961.* Toronto: Ontario
       Association of Homes for the Aged [in press].)
Peace, S.
1984   "Mental Health." In C. Nusberg. *Innovative Aging Programs Abroad.
       Implications for the United States.* Westport, Connecticut: Greenwood
       Press.
Penning, M. J., and N. L. Chappell
1980   "A Reformulation of Basic Assumptions About Institutions for the
       Elderly." In V. W. Marshall (ed.). *Aging in Canada. Social Perspectives.*
       Don Mills, Ontario: Fitzhenry and Whiteside, Ltd., 269–80.

Pfeffer, R. I., A. A. Afifi, and J. M. Chance
   1987   "Prevalence of Alzheimer's Disease in a Retirement Community."
           American Journal of Epidemiology 125(3):420–36.
Pfeiffer, E. (ed.)
   1975   *Multidimensional Functional Assessment. The OARS Methodology.*
           Durham, D. C.: Center for the Study of Aging and Human Develop-
           ment, Duke University.
Posner, J.
   1980   "Notes on the Negative Implications of Being Competent in a Home for
           the Aged." In J. Hendricks (ed.). *Institutionalization and Alternative
           Futures.* Perspectives on Aging and Human Development Series; 3.
           Farmingdale, New York: Baywood Publishing Company Inc., 138–45.
Post, F.
   1978   "The Functional Psychoses." In A. D. Isaacs and F. Post. *Studies in
           Geriatric Psychiatry.* Chichester: John Wiley and Sons, 77–94.
Preston, G. A. N.
   1986   "Dementia in Elderly Adults: Prevalence and Institutionalization." *Jour-
           nal of Gerontology* 41(2):261–67.
Price, A. L.
   1965   "Short Side Guards are Safer." *Hospital Management* 82:86, 90.
Prien, R. F., C. J. Klett, and E. M. Caffey
   1976   "Polypharmacy in the Psychiatric Treatment of Elderly Hospitalized
           Patients: A Survey of 12 Veteran's Administration Hospitals." *Diseases
           of the Nervous System* 37:333–36.
Rango, N.
   1985   "The Nursing Home Resident With Dementia: Clinical Care, Ethics, and
           Policy Implications." *Annals of Internal Medicine* 102(6):835–41.
Rapelje, D. H.
   1981   "Alternatives: How Do We Make Them Happen?" In B. T. Wigdor and
           L. Ford (eds.). *Housing for an Aging Population: Alternatives.* Proceed-
           ings of a Conference, University of Toronto, 1980, Nov. 7–8. Toronto:
           University of Toronto Press, 205–26.
Reichel, W. (ed.)
   1983   *Clinical Aspects of Aging.* Second Edition. Baltimore/London: Williams
           and Wilkins.
Reizenstein, J.
   1977   *Profile of Users. Working Paper No. 2.* CMHC Nursing Home and
           Hostels Design Guidelines Study. Ottawa, Ontario: Canada Mortgage
           and Housing Corporation.
Resnick, N. M., and S. V. Yalla
   1985   "Current Concepts: Management of Urinary Incontience in the Elderly."
           The New England Journal of Medicine 313(13):800–5.
Riportella-Muller, R., and D. P. Slesinger
   1982   "The Relationship of Ownership and Size to Quality of Care in Wiscon-
           sin Nursing Homes." *The Gerontologist* 22(4):429–34.
Robertson, D.
   1982   "Establishing New Services: Canada as a Case Study." In D. Coakley
           (ed.). *Establishing a Geriatric Service.* London and Canberra: Croom
           Helm Ltd., 199–216.

Robertson, D., R. A. Griffiths, and L. Z. Cosin
    1977   "A Community-Based Continuing Care Program for the Elderly Disabled. An Evaluation of Planned Intermittent Hospital Readmission." *Journal of Gerontology* 32(3):334–39.
Roos, N. P., E. Shapiro, and L. L. Roos
    1984   "Aging and the Demand for Health Services: Which Aged and Whose Demand?" *The Gerontologist* 24(1):31–36.
Rose, C. L., and B. Bell
    1971   *Predicting Longevity*. Lexington, Mass.: Heath Lexington Books.
Rosenthal, C. J.
    1986   "The Differentiation of Multigenerational Households." *Canadian Journal on Aging* 5(1):27–42.
Rowe, J. W.
    1985   "Health Care of the Elderly." *The New England Journal of Medicine* 312(13):827–35.
Rubenstein, L. Z., K. R. Josephson, G. D. Wieland, et al.
    1984   "Effectiveness of a Geriatric Evaluation Unit." *The New England Journal of Medicine* 311(26):1664–70.
Rubenstein, L. Z., K. R. Josephson, M. Nichol-Seamons, and A. S. Robbins
    1986   "Comprehensive Health Screening of Well Elderly Adults: An Analysis of a Community Program." *Journal of Gerontology* 41(3):342–52.
Salzman, C.
    1981   "Psychotropic Drug Use and Polypharmacy in a General Hospital. *General Hospital Psychiatry* 3:1–9.
Schafer, A.
    1985   "Restraints and the Elderly: When Safety and Autonomy Conflict." *Canadian Medical Association Journal* 132:1257–60.
Scharlach, A., and C. Frenzel
    1986   "An Evaluation of Institution-Based Respite Care." *The Gerontologist* 26(1):77–82.
Schmidt, L. J., A. M. Reinhardt, R. L. Kane, and D. M. Olsen
    1977   "Mentally Ill in Nursing Homes. New Back Wards in the Community." *Archives of General Psychiatry* 34(6):687–91.
Schneider, E. L., and J. A. Brody
    1983   "Aging, Natural Death, and Compression of Morbidity: Another View." *The New England Journal of Medicine* 309(14):854–56.
Schneider, E. L., and J. D. Reed
    1985   "Life Extension." *The New England Journal of Medicine* 312(18):1159–68.
Schneider, E. J. (Sr. Ed.), C. J. Wendlund, A. W. Zimmer, et al. (Assoc. Eds.)
    1985   *The Teaching Nursing Home: A New Approach to Geriatric Research, Education, and Clinical Care*. New York: Raven Press.
Schulz, R., and G. Brenner
    1977   "Relocation of the Aged: A Review and Theoretical Analysis." *Journal of Gerontology* 32(3):323–33.
Schuman, J. E., E. J. Beattie, D. A. Steed, et al.
    1978   "The Impact of a New Geriatric Program in a Hospital for the Chronically Ill." *Canadian Medical Association Journal* 118:639–45.

Schuman, J. E., E. J. Beattie, D. A. Steed, et al.
  1980 "Rehabilitative and Geriatric Teaching Programs: Clinical Efficacy in a Skilled Nursing Facility." *Arch. Phys. Med. Rehabil.* 61:310–15.
Schwab, Sister M.
  1983 "Professional Nursing and the Care of the Aged." In W. Reichel (ed.). *Clinical Aspects of Aging.* Second Edition. Baltimore/London: Williams and Wilkins, 564–69.
Schwenger, C. W.
  1985 "Health Care for Elderly Canadians. A New Role for Health and Welfare Canada? Summary of Conclusions and Recommendations." Unpublished typescript. Toronto, Ontario.
Schwenger, C. W., and M. J. Gross
  1980 "Institutional Care and Institutionalization of the Elderly in Canada." In V. W. Marshall (ed.). *Aging in Canada — Social Perspectives.* Don Mills, Ontario: Fitzhenry and Whiteside, 248–56.
Sehested, P., and T. Severin-Nielsen
  1977 "Falls by Hospitalized Elderly Patients: Causes, Prevention." *Geriatrics* (April):101–8.
Sellers, E. M.
  1985 "Geriatric Clinical Pharmacology." In H. Kalant, et al. (eds.). *Principles of Medical Pharmacology.* Fourth Edition. Toronto, Ontario: University of Toronto, Department of Pharmacology, 807–17.
Shanas, E.
  1971 "Measuring the Home Health Needs of the Aged in Five Countries." *Journal of Gerontology* 26(1):37–40.
Shanas, E.
  1974 "Health Status of Older People: Cross-National Implications." *American Journal of Public Health* 64(3):261–64.
Shanas, E.
  1979 "The Family as a Social Support System in Old Age." *The Gerontologist* 19(2):169–74.
Shapiro, E., and R. Tate
  1985 "Predictors of Long-Term Care Facility Use Among the Elderly." *Canadian Journal on Aging* 4(1):11–19.
Shaw, P. G.
  1982 "Common Pitfalls in Geriatric Drug Prescribing." *Drugs* 23:324–28.
Shore, H.
  1977 "New Approaches in the United States." In A. N. Exton-Smith and J. Grimley Evans (eds.). *Care of the Elderly: Meeting the Challenge of Dependency.* London: Academic Press; New York: Grune and Stratton, 121–28.
Simon, A.
  1984 "Some Observations of a Geropsychiatrist on the Value of House Calls." *The Gerontologist* 24(5):458–64.
Smith, H. L., and M. D. Fottler
  1981 "Costs and Cost Containment in Nursing Homes." *Health Services Research* 16(1):17–41.
Snyder, L. H., P. Rupprecht, J. Pyrele, et al.
  1978 "Wandering." *The Gerontologist* 18(3):272–80.

Social Planning Council of Metro Toronto
   1984   *Caring for Profit: The Commercialization of Human Services in Ontario.*
Soffer, A.
   1985   "Cost-Effective or Quality Care. Which Shall It Be?" *Archives of Internal Medicine* 145(11):1963–64.
Spitzer, W. O., D. L. Sackett, and J. C. Sibley, et al.
   1974   "The Burlington Randomized Trial of the Nurse Practitioner." *The New England Journal of Medicine* 290(5):251–56.
Statistics Canada
   1979   *1976 Census of Canada, Vol. 2, Population: Demographic Characteristics, Five-Year Age Groups, Table 11.* Ottawa: Minister of Industry, Trade and Commerce, Canada.
Statistics Canada
   1982   *1981 Census of Canada, Vol. 1, National Series, Population: Age, Sex and Marital Status, Table 1.* Ottawa: Ministry of Supply and Services Canada, Catalogue No. 92–901.
Statistics Canada
   1984(a) *List of Canadian Hospitals and Special Care Facilities, 1983, Tables 1 and 2.* Ottawa: Ministry of Supply and Services Canada, Catalogue No. 83–201.
Statistics Canada
   1984(b) *The Elderly in Canada, Table 3.* Ottawa: Ministry of Supply and Services Canada, Catalogue No. 99–932.
Statistics Canada
   1984(c) *Hospital Annual Statistics, 1981–1982, Table 4.* Ottawa: Ministry of Supply and Services Canada.
Statistics Canada
   1985   *Hospital Annual Statistics, 1982–83, Tables 1 and 2.* Ottawa: Ministry of Supply and Services Canada.
Steel, K.
   1985   "Geriatric Medicine." *Archives of Internal Medicine* 145(5):811–13.
Stoddart, G. L., and M. F. Drummond
   1984   "How to Read Clinical Journals: 7. To Understand an Economic Evaluation (Part B). *Canadian Medical Association Journal* 130 (June 15): 1542–49.
Stolee, P., K. Rockwood, and D. Robertson
   1981   *Saskatchewan Health Status Survey of the Elderly. Report I. Long-Term Care of the Elderly. Final Report.* Saskatchewan: Division of Geriatric Medicine, University of Saskatchewan.
Stolee, P., K. Rockwood, and D. Robertson
   1982   *Saskatchewan Health Status Survey of the Elderly. Report II. The Elderly in the Community. Final Report.* Saskatchewan: Division of Geriatric Medicine, University of Saskatchewan.
Stone, L. O., and S. Fletcher
   1986   *The Seniors Boom: The Dramatic Increases in Longevity and Prospects for Better Health.* Ottawa, Ontario: Ministry of Supply and Services Canada, Catalogue No. 89–515.

Strong, M. K.
    1930   Public Welfare Administration in Canada. Social Service Monographs,
            Number Ten. Chicago, Ill.: The University of Chicago Press.
Summers, W. K., L. V. Majovski, G. M. Marsh, et al.
    1986   "Oral Tetrahydroaminoacridine in Long-Term Treatment of Senile
            Dementia, Alzheimer Type." The New England Journal of Medicine
            315(20):1241–45.
Sutcliffe, B. J.
    1983   "Improving Quality of Life: Psychogeriatric Units." In M. J. Denham
            (ed.). Care of the Long-Stay Elderly Patient. London and Canberra:
            Croom Helm Ltd., 185–205.
Svanborg, A., G. Bergström, and D. Mellström
    1983   "Epidemiological Studies on Social and Medical Conditions of the
            Elderly." In EURO Reports and Studies 62, WHO Regional Office for
            Europe, Copenhagen.
Thomas, T. M., K. R. Plymat, J. Blannin, and T. W. Meade
    1980   "Prevalence of Urinary Incontinence." British Medical Journal 281:
            1243–45.
Thomson, D.
    1983   "Workhouse to Nursing Home: Residential Care of Elderly People in
            England Since 1840." Ageing and Society 3(1):43–69.
Thorson, J. A., L. Whatley, and K. Hancock
    1974   "Attitudes Towards the Aged as a Function of Age and Education." The
            Gerontologist 14(4):316–18.
Thurow, L.C.
    1985   "Medicine Versus Economics." The New England Journal of Medicine
            313(10):611–14.
Townsend, P.
    1962   The Last Refuge. A Survey of Residential Institutions and Homes for the
            Aged in England and Wales. London: Routledge and Kegan Paul.
Tribble, D. A.
    1985   "Research Needed on Cost Effectiveness of Pharmacy." American Jour-
            nal of Hospital Pharmacy 42(3):514.
Triggs, E. J., R. L. Nation, A. Long, and J. J. Ashley
    1975   "Pharmacokinetics in the Elderly." Europ. Journal of Clinical Pharma-
            cology 8:55–62.
Tucker, J. S.
    1982   "The Day Hospital." In D. Coakley (ed.). Establishing a Geriatric Ser-
            vice. London and Canberra: Croom Helm Ltd., 58–70.
Tulchinsky, T. H., P. E. Slater, and J. Menczel
    1985   "Aging: A New Public Health Challenge." Israel Journal of Medical
            Sciences 21:195–96.
Ullmann, S. G.
    1981   "Assessment of Facility Quality and Its Relationship to Facility Size in
            the Long-Term Health Care Industry." The Gerontologist 21(1):91–97.
Van Horne, R.
    1986   A New Agenda. Health and Social Service Strategies for Ontario's
            Seniors. Toronto, Ontario: Government of Ontario.

Verwoerdt, A.
1981 "Psychotherapy for the Elderly." In T. Arie (ed.). *Health Care of the Elderly*. London: Croom Helm Ltd., 118–39.

Vetter, N. J., D. A. Jones, and C. R. Victor
1981 "Urinary Incontinence in the Elderly at Home." *The Lancet* II:1275–77.

Walford, R. L.
1985 "Economic Impact of Life Span Extension." *Anti-Aging News* 5(5):49–52.

Walshe, A., and H. Rosen
1979 "A Study of Patient Falls from Bed."*Journal of Nursing Administration* (May):31–35.

Wartski, S. A., and T. H. Tulchinsky
1985 "Standards for Long-Term Care Facilities in Israel." *Israel Journal of Medical Sciences* 21:238–41.

Waterloo Region Social Resources Council and District Health Council
1985 *Home Based and Vacation Relief Services*. Unpublished discussion paper. Waterloo, Ontario.

Watson, J., P. McGibbon, J. O'Brien-Bell, et al.
1984 *Health: a Need for Redirection*. Ottawa, Ontario: Canadian Medical Association.

Wettstein, A., and R. Spiegel
1984 "Clinical Trials with the Cholinergic Drug RS86 in Alzheimer's Disease (AD) and Senile Dementia of the Alzheimer type (SDAT)." *Psychopharmacology* 84(4):572–73.

Whiting-O'Keefe, Q. E., D. W. Simborg, W. E. Epstein, and A. Warger
1985 "A Computerized Summary Medical Record System Can Provide More Information Than the Standard Medical Record." *Journal of the American Medical Association* 254(9):1185–92.

Wieland, D., L. Z. Rubenstein, J. G. Ouslander, and S. E. Martin
1986 "Organizing an Academic Nursing Home. Impacts on Institutionalized Elderly." *Journal of the American Medical Association* 255(19):2622–27.

Wilkins, R., and O. B. Adams
1983 *Healthfulness of Life — a Unified View of Mortality, Institutionalization and Non-Institutionalized Disability in Canada, 1978*. Montreal: Institute for Research on Public Policy, 25.

Williams, T. F.
1986 "Geriatrics: The Fruition of the Clinician Reconsidered." *The Gerontologist* 26(4):345–49.

Williamson, J., I. H. Stokoe, S. Gray, et al.
1964 "Old People at Home: Their Unreported Needs." *The Lancet* I:1117–20.

Willington, F. L. (ed.)
1976 *Incontinence in the Elderly*. London: Academic Press.

Wingate, L.
1984 "The Epidemiology of Osteoporosis." *Journal of Medicine* 15(4):243–66.

Wister, A. V.
1985 "Living Arrangement Choices Among the Elderly." *Canadian Journal on Aging* 4(3):127–44.

Bibliography

Wolcott, L. E.
    1983   "Rehabilitation and the Aged." In W. Reichel (ed.). *Clinical Aspects of Aging*. Second Edition. Baltimore/London: Williams and Wilkins, 182–204.
World Health Organization
    1978   "The Alma-Ata Conference on Primary Health Care." *WHO Chronicle* 32(11):409–30.
World Health Organization
    1984   "Family Support and the Elderly." *WHO Chronicle* 38(6):255.
Wurtman, R. J.
    1985   "Alzheimer's Disease." *Scientific American* 252(1):62–74.
Yarnell, J. W. G., and A. S. St. Leger
    1979   "The Prevalence, Severity and Factors Associated With Urinary Incontinence in a Random Sample of the Elderly." *Age and Ageing* 8:81–85.
Yarnell, J. W. G., G. J. Voyle, P. M. Sweetnam, et al.
    1982   "Factors Associated with Urinary Incontinence in Women." *Journal of Epidemiology and Community Health* 36:58–63.
Zorzitto, M. L., D. P. Ryan, and R. H. Fisher
    1986   "The Practice of Respite Admissions on a Geriatric Assessment Unit: The Correlates of Successful Outcome." *Canadian Journal on Aging* 5(2):105–11.
Zuckerman, Sir S.
    1969   *Medicine and Tomorrow's Community*. Glasgow, U.K.: University of Glasgow Press, Publication NS 132.

INDEX